Policy Implementation in the Federal System

Policy Implementation in the Federal System

National Goals and Local Implementors

Carl E. Van Horn
Eagleton Institute of Politics,
Rutgers University

LexingtonBooks
D.C. Heath and Company
Lexington, Massachusetts
Toronto

Library of Congress Cataloging in Publication Data

Van Horn, Carl E.
    Policy implementation in the Federal system.

    Includes index.
    1. Intergovernmental fiscal relations—United States.   2. Revenue
Sharing—United States. I. Title.
HJ275.V35   353.007'25   78-19929
ISBN 0-669-02435-x

To Gerrie

Contents

List of Figures
and Tables

Preface

Authors are fond of noting that their books address significant subjects long ignored in the literature. Not wishing to depart substantially from this noble tradition, I deal with a subject that is of critical importance to the American political system: the implementation of intergovernmental programs, especially the tension between the goals of programs promoted with federal dollars, and the realities of those programs when they are implemented by state and local elected officials.

Both implementation and intergovernmental relations have received increasing attention in recent years, but seldom have the two interests been combined. Even more rarely has more than one intergovernmental program been discussed in a single volume. This book discusses three laws that emerged from the reform movement known as the New Federalism: the State and Local Fiscal Assistance Act of 1972 (known as General Revenue Sharing), the Comprehensive Employment and Training Act of 1973, and the Housing and Community Development Act of 1974. It examines their formulation and implementation, tracing their development under successive presidential administrations and Congresses in order to learn lessons about the design of public policy and the problems of policy implementation.

The evidence, observations, and opinions offered in this book are informed by my original research on public policy implementation (most extensively on the CETA program), by the analysis of congressional hearings and agency reports, and by research conducted by others. My research on CETA was carried out over a five-year period during which I visited federal agencies in Washington, D.C., and elsewhere and traveled to over thirty state and local governments, where I interviewed elected officials, program administrators, and citizens; collected data; and observed meetings.

Policy Implementation in the Federal System is designed to serve four audiences. First, for the student of public policy, it uses an approach to the study of policy implementation which I developed in order to examine and compare the process of carrying out three significant public policies during several years and under differing national political and economic conditions.

Second, for students of intergovernmental relations and federalism, the book assesses the development, evolution, and effects of the goals embodied in the New Federalism: decentralization of authority to local elected officials, reform through program consolidation, and local accountability for program design. It also follows the changing character of these three major programs under the presidential administrations of Richard Nixon, Gerald Ford, and Jimmy Carter.

Third, for students of urban politics, it provides insight into the impact that over $100 billion in program funds has had on urban America, the poor, and minorities.

Fourth, for students of American government and politics, the book considers the relationship between legislative policy formulation and policy implementation and the implication that this relationship has for American political institutions and the shape of public policy.

Acknowledgments

In a project spanning five years, I have been fortunate to receive a great deal of financial support to conduct my research, advice from my colleagues at three institutions, and able research assistance and secretarial help. I wish to express my deep gratitude to those people who have been so generous with their time and talents.

Support for the original research reported in this book was provided by the Office of Research and Development, Employment and Training Administration, U.S. Department of Labor, by a grant from the state of Ohio, by the Mershon Center of Ohio State University, and by the Eagleton Institute of Politics of Rutgers University. Thankfully, all these institutions encourage scholars to express their opinions freely and therefore cannot be held responsible for the views expressed in these pages.

Most of the research on CETA was conducted as part of the Ohio State University—CETA Implementation Study, which began in 1974 and continues to the present. I would like to thank my colleagues on that project and especially Randall Ripley, the project's director, and Donald Baumer and Grace Franklin, two colleagues who were there from the start.

The book was written during my first year on the faculty of the Eagleton Institute. The support at Eagleton from the staff and my colleagues has been most gratifying, especially for a rookie. Cindy Schultz, Chris Lenart, and Edith Saks typed the manuscript with accuracy, dispatch, and good cheer. Fran Waldman prepared the tables and figures with her usual competence and attention to detail.

Able research assistance was provided by Anton J. Naess, Sandy Miller, and Corey Phelon. I especially want to recognize Tony Naess, however, who worked with me during the final months of manuscript preparation, demonstrating remarkable tenacity and the ability and dedication to accomplish any task I assigned to him.

Although I did not always heed their advice, I benefited from careful and insightful reviews of the entire manuscript by several very busy friends and colleagues. I am most grateful to Donald Baumer, William Gormley, Richard Lehne, Randall Ripley, Alan Rosenthal, and Cliff Zukin for their counsel. Paul Dommel and Sarah Liebschutz provided very thorough and helpful reviews of the chapter on the community development program. David Stanley Ford was most helpful in lending a "practitioner's" mind to the project, particularly in scrutinizing my chapter on CETA. Michael Reagan and David Walker provided helpful comments on a draft prospectus for this book.

The dedication is to my wife, who not only is a very supportive spouse, but also happens to be an excellent critic and a skilled editor. She shares the credit for the lucid passages in the book because she insisted that I write in English.

For any errors in fact, judgment, or mangled prose that remain, I take full responsibility.

1

Intergovernmental Policy Implementation

The widely perceived shortcomings of many Great Society programs, pressure by state and local officials for more autonomy, and the political philosophy of the Nixon administration combined to bring about reforms in intergovernmental policy in the United States during the 1970s. Those reforms, collectively dubbed the New Federalism, came about through federally funded programs that in contrast to previous narrowly defined programs were implemented under the broad authority of elected officials in states, counties, and cities.[1] State and local officials had been involved in delivering federal aid programs before, but now they were to have much more power over the central questions of public policy: who gets what, when, and how?

This book examines the legislative enactment and implementation of three programs of the New Federalism in order to determine their broad patterns of governance, program expenditures, and benefit distribution, and to study the general process of intergovernmental policy implementation. The three signal policies—the State and Local Fiscal Assistance Act of 1972 (known as General Revenue Sharing or GRS), the Comprehensive Employment and Training Act of 1973 (known as CETA), and Title I of the Housing and Community Development Act of 1974 (known as Community Development Block Grants or CDBG)—decentralized power for running the programs to state and local elected officials after broad national goals were established, but also retained, in varying degrees, federal oversight. Together the three programs now account for nearly one-fourth of the $80 billion in federal aid to state and local governments and for the vast majority of funds over which state and local elected officials have a high degree of control.[2]

Federal programs embodying national goals but administered by state and local elected officials inevitably create tensions among levels of government over the shape and content of policy. This book is about how that tension is worked out, how the politics of policy implementation influences contemporary intergovernmental policy. I have four principal objectives: first, to present a guide for the study of public policy implementation; second, to employ that framework in the analysis of three significant programs that decentralize responsibility for the achievement of national purposes to state and local levels of government; third, to examine the relationship between the politics of legislative formulation and the politics of policy

1

implementation; and fourth, to assess some of the consequences of three policies that emerged from the New Federalism era.

This chapter briefly considers the most prominent policy issues raised by the New Federalism and the three policies examined in the present study, and then outlines a framework for understanding and analyzing the implementation of intergovernmental policies.

The New Federalism

The New Federalism is best understood by reviewing the changing characteristics of intergovernmental relations over the last twenty years: it helps to know about the old federalism in order to understand what is "new" about the notion of decentralizing program control to subnational elected officials. The idea that state and local governments should be responsible for carrying out federal programs is, of course, nothing new. State and local governments have run various federally funded programs since the beginning of the republic and increasingly since the early 1950s. Aid to state and local governments expanded from $1.7 billion, or about 3 percent of the total federal budget, in fiscal year 1955[3] to $48 billion, or 15 percent of the total budget, in fiscal year 1975.[4] Growth in federal grants has been particularly sharp in the last decade, with federal assistance to state and local governments increasing from $19 billion in fiscal years 1969[5] to over $80 billion in fiscal year 1979.[6]

Throughout the long history of federal aid to state and local governments one question has always been paramount: what is the optimum distribution of responsibilities among levels of government? Individuals arguing for a strong federal role prefer the "top-down" approach to accountability, which is characterized by "specific program authorizations, . . . scrutiny of plans and applications by the federal administering agency, . . ." and ongoing oversight by federal agencies and the Congress.[7] Those who support strong state and local government endorse the "bottom-up" method of accountability, whereby officials in state and local jurisdictions may respond to their citizenry and exercise their understanding of local needs and priorities.[8] These observers doubt the capacity of distant Washington-based bureaucrats to be sensitive to local concerns because they are less accountable than local elected officials, who can be turned out of office by the voters.

The issue of what level of government should be responsible for administering the various aspects of intergovernmental policies is confronted in nearly all federal aid legislation, from welfare, education, and unemployment to health, transportation, and economic development. The degree of responsibility given to federal, state, and local governments differs with each policy and can seem confusing. Fortunately for the student of American politics, however, trends are discernible. The distribution of power in intergovernmental policy delivery resembles a swinging pendulum:[9] strong federal control will be popular with the Congress and other policymakers, then unpopular, then fashionable once again. The history of aid to state and local government over the last fifteen years can be viewed as one giant swing of this pendulum.

During the great growth period of federal grants-in-aid, the 1950s and 1960s, national assistance programs were accompanied by elaborate restrictions on the use of funds and demands that state and local governments contribute some of their resources in order to obtain the grants.[10] These features, known as the "categorical aid" approach and the "matching funds" requirements, meant that the federal government wanted to greatly influence the nature of federally funded programs mounted by state and local officials. State and local governments were viewed as a conduit through which national goals could be accomplished.

The administration of President Lyndon Johnson leaned toward strong federal control over its War on Poverty programs, which often bypassed local officials and established new delivery mechanisms such as Community Action Agencies. Johnson called his approach the "creative federalism," but it evidently did not please state and local officials, who clamored for more influence over the use of funds in their communities and states. They wanted not only money to spend but also the power to distribute it in ways they saw fit. By the 1968 presidential nominating conventions, both major political parties, with the Republicans in the lead, endorsed the concept of decentralizing more power over federal funds to states, counties, and cities. In 1969, the Nixon administration began the protracted drive to bring it about.

One of President Nixon's most important statements on intergovernmental policy was made in his 1971 State of the Union Message, in which he announced a "new American Revolution":

> The time has now come in America to reverse the flow of power and resources from the States and communities to Washington, and start power and resources flowing back from Washington to the States and communities and, more important, to the people, all across America . . . . Let us put the money where the needs are. And let us put the power to spend it where the people are.[11]

Four key elements comprised the Nixon administration's plan for the New Federalism: first, much of the decision-making power of federal agencies would be moved from Washington, D.C., to regional centers where officials committed to the new order could be appointed; second, a revenue sharing program, which would give funds to state and local governments without restrictions, would be established; third, a set of "special revenue sharing" packages would be developed to combine narrow-purpose categorical grants under omnibus block grants in such areas as education, health, housing, manpower, and transportation; and fourth, programs in natural resource management and income security would be centralized.[12]

Although President Nixon and his supporters were not successful in obtaining the entire New Federalism package, they did win significant victories in the legislative process. The three laws discussed in this volume represent different ways to accomplish President Nixon's general aim: more power to state and local officials for the design of federally funded programs. According to the U.S. Advisory Commission on Intergovernmental Relations, a bipartisan body created by the Congress in 1959 to monitor the operation of the American federal system, General Revenue Sharing, CETA, CDBG, the Partnership for Health Act, Title XX of the Social Security Act, and the Omnibus Crime Control Act (passed during the Johnson administration) are all legitimate block grants.[13] They conform to the original intentions of the New Federalism by decentralizing power to local actors and by removing many federal restrictions on the use of program funds. At their height, these block grants accounted for 23 percent of all aid to state and local government.[14]

But the pendulum is swinging again in the opposite direction: federal control has been reasserted by Congress and the Carter administration. President-elect Carter seemed to support the philosophy of the New Federalism in his first postelection news conference:

> When there's a choice to be made between the federal, state, and local levels of government to perform a function, I would prefer that the function be carried out by the level of government closest to the individual citizen.[15]

This rhetorical commitment quickly ebbed in the face of interest groups demanding federal attention to the concerns of the poor, minorities, and urban communities. President Carter transformed the New Federalism into the New Partnership, where state and local governments are involved, but with the federal government playing a leadership role. President Carter characterized one of the central shortcomings of urban programs in the 1970s:

> The Federal government retreated from its responsibilities, leaving states and localities with insufficient resources, interests or leadership to accomplish all that needed to be done. We learned that states and localities cannot solve the problems by themselves.[16]

The Carter solution called for involvement from all levels of government, the private sector, and voluntary organizations, and the reestablishment of strong federal priorities. Carter explained his position on targeting federal aid:

> I think in the past one of the major problems [has] been that when the Congress passes legislation designed to help a certain type of person or a certain type of community, quite often those services and funds have been channeled, through administrative negligence or because of political pressures, into providing services for those who don't need them nearly so much.[17]

Carter's vision of intergovernmenal policy helped bring about the return of narrow categorical programs with detailed objectives, often grafted onto block grants.

How to design policy that will both accomplish legitimate national goals and remain sensitive to legitimate local needs and priorities has been a recurring and vexing problem in American politics, for it goes to the very heart of the political process. GRS, CETA, and CDGB illustrate three similar but divergent approaches to dealing with this problem and distributing power among levels of government.

The Policies: A Brief Overview

Although each of the laws is discussed in detail in the core chapters of the book, a brief overview of their development and provisions will be presented here. Table 1-1 provides a quick summary of GRS, CETA, CDGB, and their budgetary growth.

General Revenue Sharing

The State and Local Fiscal Assistance Act of 1972 was a central component of the New Federalism package.[18] In its first five years GRS allocated nearly $30 billion to 39,000 political jurisdictions, with very few federal requirements on how the funds could be used. Local governments were limited to expenditures within nationally determined "priority expenditure categories," but these were very broad. The law required reports on planned and actual usage; it banned racial discrimination; and it prohibited using the money to match other federal grants. Otherwise, the funds could be applied to anything from tax reductions to new police cars.

GRS was revised in 1976. Among the most important changes were the removal of priority expenditure and grant matching prohibitions, inclusion of new auditing requirements, strengthening the antidiscrimination provision, and adding requirements for citizen participation—something that was not addressed in the original act.

Table 1-1

A Summary of General Revenue Sharing (GRS), the Comprehensive
Employment and Training Act (CETA), and Community Development
Block Grants (CDBG)

	GRS	CETA	CDBG
Original Public Law Number and year, and major amendments	PL92-512, 1972 PL94-488, 1976	PL93-203, 1973 PL93-567, 1974 PL94-444, 1977 PL95-524, 1978	PL93-383, 1974 PL95-128, 1977
General Purpose	Financial aid to state and local governments	Training programs, and public service employment	The development of viable urban areas, elimination of slums and blight
Recipient Units	Over 39,000 general purpose governments	Over 450 prime sponsorships: places with 100,000 population or more and states	Over 4,500 metropolitan areas, nonmetropolitan areas, and states
Budget Information (in billions)			
First year's amount[b]	$ 5.3	$ 3.4[a]	$ 2.5
Fiscal year 1978	$ 6.7	$ 7.3	$ 3.5
Total funds, year 1 to fiscal year 1978	$43.4	$23.1	$11.9
Percent increase from year 1 to fiscal year 1978	26%	115%	40%

Sources: GRS: U.S. Department of the Treasury, Office of Revenue Sharing, First through Sixth Annual Reports, 1973-1979.
CETA: Congressional Research Service, *The Comprehensive Employment and Training Act as Amended by PL95-524* (CRS Report Number 78-252 E.P.W., December 10, 1978, p. CRS-8).
CDBG: U.S. Department of Housing and Urban Development, *Community Development Block Grants, Directory of Allocations for FY '78* (Washington, D.C.: Government Printing Office, 1978), p. vii.

[a]The CETA budget data includes Titles I, II, VI, and all special and summer youth programs that are run by local government. Nationally run programs were omitted.

[b]GRS's first year ran from January to December 1972. CETA's first year was fiscal year 1975 (July 1974 to June 1975). CDBG's first year was fiscal year 1975.

*The Comprehensive Employment
and Training Act*

CETA[19] eliminated seventeen federally managed categorical programs authorized over a ten-year period, replacing them with a broad block grant for the creation of "comprehensive manpower services," in the language of the statute. Initially a training program oriented toward low-income individuals, CETA became a tool to serve temporarily unemployed workers affected by the recession of the late 1970s. Its budget expanded substantially in only a few years, from $3.4 billion to $7.3 billion per year.

Funds were dispensed to over 450 units of local government with populations of 100,000 or more and to all fifty states. Known as "prime sponsors" in the act, they may directly run virtually any training or employment program or may subcontract to community and educational agencies. Each eligible political jurisdiction received some benefits directly or indirectly: no matching monies were required. The law had a complex set of rules for who could enroll in CETA programs. Overall initial requirements were quite broad but gradually became more restrictive, so that by the 1978 revision of the law long-term unemployed and low-income individuals were the only clients of the program. The law directed state and local government officials to appoint a Manpower Planning Council, composed of community representatives, which would advise elected officials. Final authority for how the funds were spent rested with the chief elected officials, but the federal Department of Labor held approval power over local plans and evaluated prime sponsors' performance.

CETA was amended several times between 1973 and 1978. In general the revisions tended either to expand the scope of CETA's activities or place additional restrictions on the way funds could be used and the people who should benefit from them.

Community Development Block Grants

Title I of the Housing and Community Development Act of 1974, known as Community Development Block Grants (CDBG),[20] supplied grants for the improvement of urban communities through a variety of programs ranging from physicial redevelopment to social services. It eliminated seven grant-in-aid programs that had been enacted over the preceding twenty-five years.

An average of $3 billion per year was allocated by formula to most large political jurisdictions. Discretionary grants were made available to smaller areas. Following the precedent established by CETA, CDBG listed several national goals that local governments were to consider when allocating their CDBG funds, but specific priorities were not mandated. Projects were permitted to benefit the entire community, but, according to the law, "maximum feasible priority should be given to low- or moderate-income families . . . ." CDBG required assurances from recipients that they would hold public hearings. Under CDBG the federal government's role was reduced in comparison with the categorical period, but it still had responsibility for program monitoring and evaluation.

The reauthorization of CDBG in 1977 made minor changes in its overall structure and purpose. Perhaps its most important amendment altered the formula for distributing the funds in such a way as to benefit cities in the older areas of the Northeast. The new law also strengthened requirements for citizen participation and added to the general block grant a categorical grant for severely distressed urban areas.

GRS, CETA, and CDBG shared the common theme of decentralization, yet each represented a different compromise between competing interests in the Congress, the administration, state and local governments, and interest groups. State and local elected officials gained substantial control over the implementation of national goals, but federal oversight was retained. Narrow standards for the distribution of benefits were initially absent from all policies, but national goals for helping low-income people surfaced in CETA and CDBG and eventually were required in CETA. Potential local checks on the power of local elected officials were inserted through various mechanisms for citizen participation that ranged from formal advisory boards in CETA to public hearings in CDBG and the 1976 version of GRS. The laws articulate national goals, most unambiguously in the case of CETA and very loosely in General Revenue Sharing. Officials in autonomous state and local jurisidctions must interpret and carry out these goals. The language of the acts allows federal, state, and local actors extraordinary discretion over the design of programs, the types of individuals who should benefit from them, and the relationships that should be effected among levels of government and within communities and states.

An Approach to the Study of Intergovernmental Policy Implementation

Enactment of the New Federalism legislation only temporarily resolved the policy issues involved. Because the laws' legislative intent was frequently vague and sometimes internally inconsistent, the problems of implementing them, of assembling the necessary resources and political support to carry them out, loomed large. Especially because GRS, CETA, and CDBG represented attempts at a major departure from the previous structure of federal grant programs, the process of implementing them was likely to be most difficult and interesting.

Some scholars have noted that statutes are analogous to theories.[21] They contain many assumptions about the way the world works (in this case the intergovernmental system), but the real test of the theory or statute comes when agencies and state and local officials attempt to carry out the law—expectations must be measured, tested, and reexamined in the light of experience. Indeed, there will frequently be a significant gap between the goals and purposes of the policymakers and the actual delivery of public services. As Kenneth Dolbeare and Phillip Hammond argue:

> Very little may really be decided by the words of a decision or a statute: the enunciation of such national policy may be just the beginning of the decisive process of determining what will happen to whom, and understanding this further stage is essential to a full understanding of politics.[22]

Following their suggestion, the present study assesses both the legislative history of the three laws and the process of putting legislative goals and aspirations into practice in state and local governments.

Increasingly policy analysts are recognizing the importance of implementation and turning their attention to it in such areas as education, welfare, housing, economic development, air pollution, employment and training, and community development.[23] These studies have identified important influences on the process of policy implementation; however, most of them provide no coherent framework for analysis, and those that do offer conceptual frameworks seldom link them with specific case study examinations.[24] The results have been twofold. First, there are a wealth of good case studies whose findings seem idiosyncratic because the explanations and variables chosen are tailored exclusively for the single case under investigation. Second, the analytic frameworks are almost never systematically applied to more than one policy, and often are not applied at all. The approach to the study of policy implementation presented in this volume will guide the assessment of GRS, CETA, and CDBG and, I hope, lead to broader generalizations about the process of intergovernmental policy implementation.[25] Let us begin with some useful definitions and distinctions.

It is important to distinguish between *policy implementation* and what is often referred to as *policy impact*. Policy implementation encompasses actions by public and private individuals or groups that affect the achievement of objectives set forth in prior policy decisions. The student of policy implementation examines the process of putting policy statements into public services through federal, state, and local administrative agencies. Implementation research determines whether those public services were delivered as they were intended, and whether the changes in program structure and operation mandated by the statute occurred. The tasks of this form of policy analysis are, first, to measure the proximate effects of public policy[26]—for example, whether the intended recipients of CETA training actually receive it; and second, to understand the organizational, political, and economic factors that produced or hindered the observed results. Implementation research should be designed to ask both "what happened . . . [and] why did it happen this way?"[27]

Policy impact studies typically examine a different but also profoundly important set of questions by focusing on the policy's ultimate effect on society or its beneficiaries. For example, such studies might assess the extent to which the wages of low-income people were affected by enrollment in CETA programs, or the extent to which blighting conditions were actually arrested or eliminated by CDBG.

A central difference between policy implementation and policy impact research is that the former is perhaps more modest in its aspirations, though no less important. Answering the questions posed by implementation research is necessary so that policymakers and citizens can evaluate the efficacy of public policies. One needs to know whether the programs designed by policymakers were the programs that were actually delivered. And, in order to make effective recommendations for change, analysts must know not only what happened, but why. Nevertheless, implementation research stops short of addressing the more difficult questions of whether the policy really improved the general problems it was designed to meet. Policies may be fully implemented but fail to have positive effects on individuals or society's ills for a variety of reasons ranging from poorly conceived policies to the possibility that the problems at which it was aimed were intractable. A successful implementation effort is usually a necessary, but not a sufficient, condition for the production of positive ultimate impacts: the right people may get the service you want to give them, but it may not make any difference. Of course, a policy may have some positive effects, even if it is poorly implemented.

Program Performance: What Happened?

The approach to policy implementation analysis utilized here is not designed to evaluate the ultimate impact of intergovernmental programs. Rather it seeks to describe and explain what I call *program performance*, or what I referred to earlier as the proximate effects of GRS, CETA, and CDBG. My analysis is directed at determining the consequences of the New Federalism's managerial and political goals—decategorization of grants and decentralization of decision-making—and the degree to which programs and services provided for by law are delivered to the intended beneficiaries.

The selection of criteria for assessing a law's program performance is a crucial stage in analyzing implementation: the performance measures are used to assess whether or not the law's goals are realized. The definition of implementation favored here implies that it is virtually impossible to undertake an evaluation of policy implementation without first understanding its goals. But the task of identifying the goals of public policy is often very difficult. Policymakers may be intentionally vague; their goals may be conflicting and inconsistent, hard to discern or unstated.

The problems of determining a policy's goals do not mean that it is impossible to study implementation. Rather, the researcher must choose some goals against which to evaluate performance, relying on the statements of participants in the legislative process, the statute itself, the regulations and guidelines accompanying the law, or criteria suggested by client groups or specialists in the field.

Different analysts may select different goals or questions to evaluate. This book does not provide a comprehensive overview of the three laws: one must be selective, ignoring some questions and focusing on others. Students interested in a detailed and thorough examination of GRS, CETA, and CDBG must examine the works cited in the references of each chapter. Instead of presenting full-blown case studies this volume investigates a substantial number of the major policy issues raised by the statutes, concentrating on three areas of program performance.

Who Governs? The relationship between federal government overseers and state and local officials, and the role of elected officials and citizens in decision-making.

How Are the Funds Spent? The kinds of programs funded and the degree to which these programs depart from past practices.

Who Benefits? The types of people that receive program benefits and how this relates to the intent of the laws.

Who Governs? Perhaps the most difficult issue faced by policymakers during the development of GRS, CETA, and CDBG was determining the degree of power that should be granted to various levels of government by the statutes. The laws lodge primary decision-making responsibility with state and local elected officials or chief administrative officers and prescribe various degrees of federal direction and oversight. Power is shared between levels of government; gray areas are abundant.

Proponents of the New Federalism claimed that decentralization would increase accountability for decisions and enhance citizen influence over the use of federal monies. According to President Nixon, "The crucial question is not where the money comes from, but whether the official who spends it can be made to answer to those who are affected by the choices he makes."[28] The Nixon administration architects of GRS, CETA, and CDBG did not request specific mechanisms for citizen input at the local level, but some members of Congress feared that, without it, conservative local groups would have disproportionate influence over the allocation of resources. They hoped that mandating attention to citizens under CETA and CDBG would help insure accountability and strengthen community groups, such as the poor, that the federal government had nurtured, often over the objections of local officials. The legislation, however, did not require local officials to heed citizen advice, nor did it insist that the poor be prominently represented.

The following chapters examine the nature and patterns of influence among elected officials, citizens, and the federal government in the implementation of GRS, CETA, and CDBG. In short, the question is who participates in decision-making and what difference does it make?

How Are the Funds Spent? Another central issue in the development of these policies was the need to design programs responsive to local needs and circumstances. Nearly all participants in the legislative process agreed that categorical aid programs were overly restrictive, asserting national models for programs that were often inappropriate if not pernicious for state and local jurisdictions. None of these policies wipes the slate clean: federal preferences are stated for how the funds should be used, but the degree of national control is considerably relaxed in all three, even though GRS, CETA, and CDBG outline national priorities.

The ways in which state and local officials take advantage of this increased authority for assigning funds to programs that they value, and how their choices differ from the results of the categorical era, are assessed in the chapters that follow.

Who Benefits? During the struggle to enact New Federalism laws, opponents of decentalization feared that giving more power to state and local officials would mean less resources for cities, minorities, and the poor.[29] A report by an advisory committee to the U.S. Department of Housing and Urban Development proposed that "special revenue sharing programs" require that "allocated funds (or certain percentages of them) . . . be used to redress the effects of racial and economic disadvantage."[30] Congress did not heed the committee's suggestion in the original versions of GRS, CETA, or CDBG. CETA and CDBG urged attention to low-income groups, but did not reserve funds for them.

Shapers of the New Federalism policies debated bitterly over who should benefit and how much control should be granted to local officials to make this decision. Those favoring strict targeting of federal aid to low-income people cited a political rationale: the poor are not politically powerful in general and they are even less powerful at the local level than they are at the national level.[31] Proponents of tight federal guidelines dwelled upon the likes of the Director of Human Resources in Little Rock, Arkansas, who attemped to explain a CDBG-funded tennis court by noting: "You can't divorce politics from that much money. . . . We must remember the needs of the people who vote . . . because they hold us accountable. . . . Poor people don't vote.''[32] Proponents of continued federal control did not want to remand the stewardship of the disadvantaged to state and local elected officials.

Less passionate critics offered a different reason, maintaining that restrictive federal aid requirements on who should benefit from programs provide state and local politicians with an essential scapegoat that justifies spending money on the poor.[33] In the opinion of Mayor Moon Landrieu of New Orleans, "Categorical programs made it possible and politically feasible to concentrate dollars in poorer sections of the nation's cities."[34]

Individuals and groups who wanted to remove federal constraints on who benefits from federal grants countered that state and local governments had served the poor in the past and would continue to do so. They also recalled that categorical programs with specific requirements for the distribution of benefits, such as Title I of the Elementary and Secondary Education Act, had not always been successful in getting money to those the legislation intended to reach.[35]

In the end, the two sides compromised. The legislation that emerged eliminated narrowly defined eligibility standards but espoused national goals favoring the poor. The empirical question is what share of the resoures do low-income and minority groups receive under GRS, CETA, and CDBG? The analysis examines evidence on the *direct* benefits to these groups, rather than indirect benefits that might be derived from the overall economic improvement and stability of middle- and upper-income groups. For instance, GRS, CETA, and CDBG indirectly benefit low-income groups when they improve the general environment of the community and even when funds go to middle-income groups. Such indirect benefits will be used in the overall assessment of the policies, but the principal focus is on examining the immediate tangible outcomes of the programs.[36]

In summary, the indicators of program performance help gauge the effects of GRS, CETA, and CDBG. Whether stated or not, the laws assume that decentralizing responsibility for decision-making will alter the relationship between levels of government and the poltical process within communities. Moreover, one of the fundamental reasons for passing those statutes was the hope that new approaches to coping with old problems would be advanced by state and local governments. Finally, the laws in various ways suggest national concern for low-income people; participants in the legislative process made divergent predictions about what level of benefits the poor would receive under the new laws. The evaluation of program performance assesses the degree to which the assumptions of lawmakers and interest groups were justified empirically.

Explaining Program Performance:
Why Did It Happen This Way?

The analysis of policy implementation involves two stages. First program performance for GRS, CETA, and CDBG will be described according to the general areas outlined above. Then, broad explanations for those outcomes will be derived by examining the series of intervening events and conditions posited by the model of policy implementation in figure 1-1. The model helps structure our understanding of the implementation process by grouping a number of complex attitudes, relationships, and conditions into general sets of factors that influence program performance. Three variable clusters will be considered in my evaluation of GRS, CETA, and CDBG: first, the *policy standards and resources*—the statute and the funds it provides; second, the *national policy environment*—federal level administrators, elected officials, and national organizations who attempt to exert influence over policy implementation; and third, the *local policy environment*—the attitudes and influence of politicians, administrators, citizens, and interest groups in the states and communities where the program operates; the social, economic, and fiscal condition of those areas; and the characteristics of the agency that is responsible for carrying out the law. What follows is a brief definition and elaboration of each category.

Policy Standards and Resources. The law and its resources influence the nature of program performance by providing a beginning point for negotiation among participants in the intergovernmental system, resources for program administration, and criteria by which federal officials, interest groups, and the courts may judge and attempt to influence state and local government behavior in relation to the legislation's goals.

The importance of resources to any program does not require much elaboration: inadequate funds are almost always cited as a reason for the failure of implementation efforts. But there are two other aspects of program resources that will also be considered in the analysis of the three laws, namely, the timing of the funds and the size of those funds in relation to the overall budget of the community. The way in which program funds are used depends in large part on when they are available for use by state or local government officials and whether they represent a significant enlargement of total resources or only a small increment.

Another important dimension in this category is the policy's statements of intent. Found in diverse sources, but principally in the law itself, the policy's standards (procedures, prohibitions, priorities) help account for variations in the power of federal, state, and local agencies and in their in-

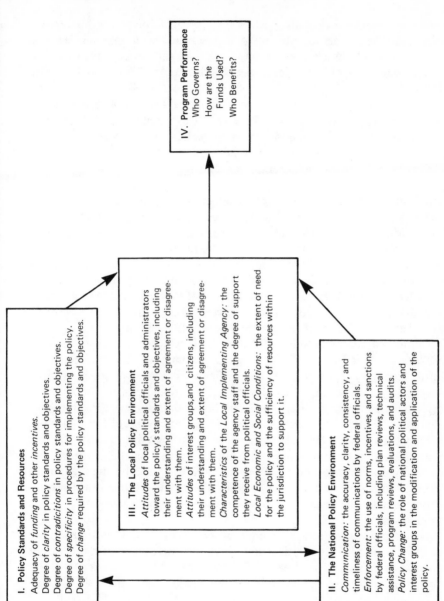

I. Policy Standards and Resources

Adequacy of *funding* and other *incentives.*
Degree of *clarity* in policy standards and objectives.
Degree of *contradicitions* in policy standards and objectives.
Degree of *specificity* in procedures for implementing the policy.
Degree of *change* required by the policy standards and objectives.

II. The National Policy Environment

Communication: the accuracy, clarity, consistency, and timeliness of communications by federal officials.
Enforcement: the use of norms, incentives, and sanctions by federal officials, including plan reviews, technical assistance, program reviews, evaluations, and audits.
Policy Change: the role of national political actors and interest groups in the modification and application of the policy.

III. The Local Policy Environment

Attitudes of local political officials and administrators toward the policy's standards and objectives, including their understanding and extent of agreement or disagreement with them.
Attitudes of interest groups, and citizens, including their understanding and extent of agreement or disagreement with them.
Characteristics of the *Local Implementing Agency:* the competence of the agency staff and the degree of support they receive from political officials.
Local Economic and Social Conditions: the extent of need for the policy and the sufficiency of resources within the jurisdiction to support it.

IV. Program Performance

Who Governs?
How are the Funds Used?
Who Benefits?

Figure 1-1. A Model of Intergovermental Policy Implementation

terpretations of policy goals. GRS, CETA, and CDBG will be analyzed to determine the degree of ambiguity and contradiction in their standards. If the policy standards are inconsistent, confusing, and unclear, one would expect a wide range of responses to the policy by federal, state, and local officials.

In summary, my analysis of the three laws will examine the characteristics of the policies and the extent to which they are altered by amendments. Such information will help explain the responses of federal, state, and local elected officials and administrators to the legislation, and their role in the implementation process.

The National Policy Environment. The policy serves as a base, but it must be interpreted, communicated, and enforced by federal agencies responsible for its administration. The general category of the national policy environment encompasses the potential influence of national level actors on the implementation process. Three elements of this environment will be incorporated into the analysis: the communication and interpretation of policy by federal administrators, the enforcement of policy by those individuals, and the influence of national level interest groups and policymakers on those federal administrative agencies and policy positions.

Policy standards cannot be followed by local level officials unless they are communicated with sufficient clarity; yet communication between levels of the federal system is complex and difficult. Federal government agencies may distort the intent of the policy either intentionally or unintentionally, or provide conflicting statements over time. Contradictory directives may also come from different sources in the federal bureaucracy. The analysis of GRS, CETA, and CDBG will assess the accuracy, clarity, consistency, and timeliness of the information transmitted by the federal administering agency in comparison with the policy's standards. Also, the investigation of federal communication with state and local officials will reveal which goals (from among the many that could be given prominence) are in fact emphasized.

Once policy standards are communicated, they must be enforced. Since there is no hierarchy of officials in the intergovernmental system that can be ordered to "comply" with national policy, federal level implementors rely on a variety of methods to influence the actions of state and local implementors. Among the techniques most commonly employed are appealing to professional norms of performance; providing technical assistance and political support; specifying elaborate procedural requirements and assurances from recipients; conducting on-site audits, program reviews, and evaluations; and threatening to withhold or actually withholding funds from state and local agencies. The various enforcement methods of federal officials will also be utilized in building an explanation for the responses of local officials. Such an examination is especially important for GRS, CETA, and CDBG because they were designed to lessen federal control.

Interactions among national political actors are also important to the implementation process because these interactions help determine the interpretation and enforcement of existing policy as well as the shape of future policy. The key participants in the national policy environment include the federal agency or agencies responsible for overseeing the policy, the White House staff (the Office of Management and Budget and, very rarely, the president), the Congress (leaders of the House and Senate committees and subcommittees responsible for policy formulation, appropriations, and oversight; members of Congress drawn into the process by local political officials; and, occasionally, the entire Congress), and national interest groups (especially groups representing state and local government officials, such as the National League of Cities, the U.S. Conference of Mayors, the National Association of Counties, and the National Governors Association, and other organizations concerned with the formulation and implementation of the law).

National political actors (excluding the federal implementing agency) can affect implementation by intervening in specific decisions by the federal agency on behalf of constituent groups, by commenting upon and even drafting regulations, and by pressuring federal agencies to administer the law in accord with their clientele's preferences. Finally, these groups play major roles in amending legislation and interpreting program performance to policymakers. Analysis of their role is essential for understanding the dynamics of policy change and the direction of policy implementation.

The Local Policy Environment. This category consists of the attitudes of officials responsible for program implementation in states and communities and the attitudes and influence of citizens and interest groups. Also included are the characteristics of the agency charged with handling the program, and conditions of the local economy and government finances. Naturally, since the study focuses on laws that decentralize power to state and local governments, these factors will play a major part in determining program performance.

The attitudes of local political officials and administators make up the first component of the local policy environment. The success or failure of many federal grant programs has been attributed to the level of support for the programs and to the policy preferences of those responsible for carrying them out. Three elements of the officials' responses will affect their willingness to follow federal policy: understanding the policy's goals, the extent of agreement or disagreement with them, and the extent to which current practices must be altered.

The attitudes of citizens and interest groups are separated from the previous category because they have an independent influence on the implementation process, apart from the influence of officials who run the programs. Their support for or opposition to a policy and the demands they make on elected officials and agency heads who make program decisions can be very important in accounting for program performance.

The formal and informal characteristics of the local implementing agency affect its ability to carry out policy: no matter what the attitudes of its personnel, the agency's structure and relations with other officials and units of government will influence the prospects for effective implementation. Among the factors that will be examined here are the experience and competence of the agency's staff, the status of the agency within the local government structure, and its financial and political support.

Finally, local economic and social conditions influence program performance by affecting the willingness of officials to embrace or reject the policy's goals and by affecting the uses to which the funds are put. For example, communities under severe fiscal pressure will allocate their grant money in ways very different from those of states and communities under little or no fiscal pressure.

Taken together, the policy standards and resources, the national policy environment, and the local policy environment help explain program performance—who governs, how are the funds spent, and who benefits from the programs? Each set of variables will be employed in building an understanding of GRS, CETA, and CDBG.

Organization of the Study

The subsequent chapters on General Revenue Sharing, CETA, and Community Development Block Grants follow a common outline, first presenting the legislative history and major amendments to the laws, then describing program performance, and, finally, attempting to account for program performance by applying the model of policy implementation. The principal justification for this highly structured outline is to facilitate systematic comparisons of experience under the three laws so that generalizations about the process of intergovernmental implementation can be developed. Chapter 5 compares the patterns of program performance and the factors that seem to determine it and considers the implications for our understanding of policy implementation and the design of intergovernmental policy.

Notes

1. Early discussions and assessments of the New Federalism may be found in Michael D. Reagan, *The New Federalism* (New York: Oxford

Univ. Press, 1972); Joseph D. Sneed and Steven A. Waldhorn, eds., *Restructuring the Federal System Approaches to Accountability in Postcategorical Programs* (New York: Crane, Russak & Co., 1975); Walter F. Scheffer, ed., *General Revenue Sharing and Decentralization* (Norman: Univ. of Oklahoma Press, 1975); and Wallace E. Oates, ed., *Financing the New Federalism* (Baltimore: Johns Hopkins Press, 1975).

2. U.S., Executive Office of the President, Office of Management and Budget, *Special Analyses, Budget of the United States Government, Fiscal Year 1979* (Washington, D.C.: Government Printing Office, 1978) (hereafter *Budget of the United States, Fiscal Year 1979*).

3. Henry Owens and Charles L. Schultze, eds., *Setting National Priorities: The Next Ten Years* (Washington, D.C.: The Brookings Institution, 1976), pp. 328, 333.

4. U.S., Congress, General Accounting Office, *Changing Patterns of Federal Aid to State and Local Governments 1969-75* (Washington, D.C., December 20, 1975), p. 2.

5. Ibid.

6. *Budget of the United States, Fiscal Year 1979*.

7. U.S., Advisory Commission on Intergovernmental Relations, *The Comprehensive Employment and Training Act: Early Readings from a Hybrid Block Grant* (Washington, D.C.: Government Printing Office, 1977), p. 12.

8. Ibid.

9. Herbert Kaufman, "Administrative Decentralization and Political Power," *Public Administration Review* 29 (1969):3-15.

10. For an excellent history of the categorical era see Reagan, *The New Federalism*.

11. U.S., Congress, House, *Miscellaneous Documents*, Vol. 1-1, 92nd Cong., 1st sess., pp. 4-5.

12. See Richard P. Nathan, "Federalism and Fiscal Relations," *Annals* 419 (May 1975):124.

13. U.S., Advisory Commission on Intergovernmental Relations, *Block Grants: A Roundtable Discussion* (Washington, D.C.: Government Printing Office, 1976), p. ii.

14. Owens and Schultze, eds., *Setting National Priorities*, p. 360.

15. "Transcript of a News Conference Held by President-Elect Carter in Georgia," *New York Times* 16 November 1976, pp. 32-33.

16. "Excerpts from the President's Message to Congress Outlining His Urban Policy," *New York Times* 28 March 1978.

17. Rochelle L. Stanfield, "Is the Man from Georgia Ready to Help the States and Cities?" *National Journal Reports* 9 (1977):138.

18. An excellent legislative history of General Revenue Sharing may be found in Paul R. Dommel, *The Politics of Revenue Sharing* (Bloomington: Indiana Univ. Press, 1974).

19. For background on CETA see Roger Davidson, *The Politics of*

Comprehensive Manpower Legislation (Baltimore: Johns Hopkins Press, 1972); and Sar A. Levitan and Joyce K. Zickler, *The Quest for a Workable Federal Manpower Partnership* (Cambridge, Mass.: Harvard Univ. Press, 1974).

20. For background information on CDBG see U.S., Advisory Commission on Intergovernmental Relations, *Community Development: The Workings of a Federal-Local Block Grant* (Washington, D.C.: Government Printing Office, 1977).

21. Jeffrey L. Pressman and Aaron B. Wildavsky, *Implementation* (Berkeley: Univ. of California Press, 1973).

22. Kenneth M. Dolbeare and Phillip E. Hammond, *The School Prayer Decision: From Court Policy to Local Practice* (Chicago: Univ. of Chicago Press, 1971), p. 149.

23. See, for example, Stephen K. Bailey and Edith K. Mosher, *ESEA: The Office of Education Administers a Law* (Syracuse: Syracuse Univ. Press, 1968); Jerome T. Murphy, *State Education Agencies and Discretionary Funds: Grease the Squeaky Wheel* (Lexington, Mass.: Lexington Books, D.C. Heath and Company, 1974); Martha Derthick, *The Influence of Federal Grants: Public Assistance in Massachusetts* (Cambridge, Mass.: Harvard Univ. Press, 1970); Martha Derthick, *New Towns In-Town* (Washington, D.C.: The Urban Institute, 1972); Pressman and Wildavsky, *Implementation*; Charles O. Jones, *Clean Air: The Policies and Politics of Pollution Control* (Pittsburgh: Univ. of Pittsburgh Press, 1975); Randall B. Ripley et al., *The Implementation of CETA in Ohio*, R & D Monograph No. 44, Employment and Training Administration, U.S. Department of Labor (Washington, D.C.: Government Printing Office, 1977); and Paul R. Dommel et al., *Decentralizing Community Development* (Washington, D.C.: Government Printing Office, 1978).

24. See, for example, Eugene Bardach, *The Implementation Game: What Happens after a Bill Becomes a Law?* (Cambridge, Mass.: MIT Press, 1977); Erwin C. Hargrove, *The Missing Link: The Study of the Implementation of Social Policy* (Washington, D.C.: The Urban Institute, 1975); Martin Rein and Francine F. Rabinowitz, "Toward a Theory of Implementation" (mimeo, 1976); Donald S. Van Meter and Carl E. Van Horn, "The Policy Implementation Process: A Conceptual Framework," *Administration and Society* 6 (1975):445-488; and Richard F. Elmore," Organizational Models of Social Program Implementation," *Public Policy* 26 (1978):185-228.

25. Carl E. Van Horn and Donald S. Van Meter, "The Implementation of Intergovernmental Policy," in Charles O. Jones and Robert D. Thomas, eds., *Public Policy-Making in a Federal System*, Vol. 3, Sage Yearbooks in Politics and Public Policy (Beverly Hills: Sage Publications, 1976), presents a much different version of the model utilized here.

26. Robert A. Levine, "Policy Analysis and Economic Opportunity Programs," in U.S. Congress, Joint Economic Committee, *The Analysis and Evaluation of Public Expenditures*, 90th Cong., 1st sess., Vol. 3, 1969, p. 1190.

27. Kenneth M. Dolbeare, "The Impact of Public Policy," in Cornelius P. Cotter, ed., *Political Science Annual: An International Review, Volume 5* (Indianapolis: Bobbs-Merrill Co., 1974).

28. "Revenue Sharing Message," *Weekly Compilation of Presidential Documents* 7 (8 February 1971):169.

29. Michael D. Reagan, "The Pro and Con Arguments," *Annals* 419 (May 1975):29.

30. Subcommittee on the Planning Process and Urban Development, Advisory Committee to the U.S. Department of Housing and Urban Development, *Revenue Sharing and the Planning Process: Shifting the Locus of Responsibility for Domestic Problem Solving* (Washington, D.C.: National Academy of Sciences, 1974), p. 59.

31. See, for example, Reagan, *The New Federalism*, p. 75; and Phillip Moneypenny, "Federal Grants in-Aid to State Governments," *National Tax Journal* 3 (1960):1-16.

32. Raymond Brown, Ann Coil, and Carol Rose, *A Time for Accounting: The Housing and Community Development Act in the South* (Atlanta: The Southern Regional Council, 1976), p. 53.

33. See, for example, Subcommittee on the Planning Process, *Revenue Sharing*, p. 58; and Bernard J. Frieden and Marshall Kaplan, "Community Development and the Model Cities Legacy," Working Paper No. 42 (Cambridge, Mass.: Joint Center for Urban Studies of the Massachusetts Institute of Technology and Harvard University, mimeo, 1976), pp. 17, 34.

34. *National Journal Reports* 4 (1972):1923.

35. See, for example, Charles Brecher, *The Impact of Federal Anti-Poverty Policies* (New York: Praeger, 1973); and Reagan, "The Pro-Con Arguments," p. 27.

36. See Robert L. Lineberry, *Equality and Urban Policy: The Distribution of Municipal Public Services* (Beverly Hills: Sage Publications, 1977); and Frank S. Levy, Arnold J. Meltsner, and Aaron B. Wildavsky, *Urban Outcomes* (Berkeley: Univ. of California Press, 1974).

2 General Revenue Sharing

The State and Local Fiscal Assistance Act of 1972, known as General Revenue Sharing (GRS), appropriated over $30 billion in federal aid to 39,000 state and local governments during its first five years. Reauthorized for another forty-five months in 1976 to allocate another $25 billion, GRS is the largest single program of federal assistance to state and local governments. Because the shared revenues are distributed with limited federal direction and no explicit statements of national goals and priorities, GRS has been the focus of debate ever since its enactment. Critics assailed it as the "biggest giveaway program ever enacted,"[1] while state and local officials praised it as "the best thing since ice cream."[2] Given these diverse interpretations of GRS's purposes and goals, it is especially important to examine its legislative history.

A Legislative History of General Revenue Sharing

GRS has engendered controversy primarily because the concept of "revenue sharing" means different things to different people. Strictly speaking, it refers to a procedure by which one governmental unit shares a fixed amount of its revenue with another unit of government.[3] In fact, General Revenue Sharing does not even meet this criterion because the program's funds were not tied to a percentage of federal revenues, but appropriated in the legislation.

In the nineteenth century the federal government enacted revenue sharing programs to assist state and local jurisdictions and to reduce national revenue surpluses. The Surplus Distribution Act of 1836 allocated all federal funds in the United States Treasury in excess of $5 million to the states, with little or no supervision of their use exercised by the federal government. The practice of unrestricted grants was abandoned in 1862, however, when Congress authorized the Morrill Act, giving land to the states for the express purpose of establishing higher education institutions.[4]

The legislative history of General Revenue Sharing spans over two decades. Early support for the revenue sharing idea developed in the 1950s and 1960s. Major congressional action began in earnest after the election of Richard Nixon in 1969, culminating in the original statute in 1972. The law was reauthorized in 1976. Each period in the law's development will be briefly discussed below, emphasizing the original statute and its implementation.

During the fifteen-year period leading up to the enactment of GRS, over 100 bills proposing some form of revenue sharing were introduced in Congress.[5] Because the concept of sharing federal funds with state and local governments can encompass conservative or liberal values,[6] it was popular among liberals and conservatives, Republicans and Democrats, and officials at all levels of government. As Michael Reagan has pointed out, "The single greatest appeal of revenue sharing is that *on the surface* it appears to combine both the liberal desire for an enlarged public sector, and the conservative desire to avoid further enlargement" (emphasis added).[7]

Conservative supporters of revenue sharing promoted the idea because they felt it would increase the power of state and local governments, reduce the influence of federal bureaucrats, restrain the growth of the national government, replace categorical grant programs, and increase administrative efficiency.[8] A bill embodying the conservative approach was introduced by Representative Melvin Laird (R.-Wis.) as early as 1958.

Liberal supporters based their proposals on a different foundation. They felt that revenue sharing could help solve urban financial stress, substitute federal income taxes for state and local government property and sales taxes, expand the provision of public services, modernize state and local governments, and assist low-income residents of the nation's cities. One proposal incorporating some of these ideas was made in 1964 by Walter Heller, chairman of the Council of Economic Advisors during the Johnson administration, and Joseph Pechman of the Brookings Institution. The Heller-Pechman plan would have redistributed aid from richer to poorer regions of the nation and increased reliance on the federal income tax. Their plan was never advanced by President Johnson because it was to have been financed from an expected $6 billion surplus of federal funds which disappeared as soon as the Vietnam war expanded.[9]

In short, the revenue sharing proposals of the 1950s and 1960s espoused divergent political philosophies. Democrats and liberals wanted to redistribute income; Republicans and conservatives wanted to give some of Washington's power to state and local officials and thereby trim the national government's influence over local decisions.

The revenue sharing concept favored by many conservatives, Republicans, and state and local officials was given a boost by the election of Richard Nixon.[10] Shortly after taking office in 1969, he introduced a revenue sharing bill to send $500 million to the states. Outlining his proposal, President Nixon said that the funds would be distributed "with a minimum of Federal restrictions on how those dollars are to be used, and with a requirement that a percentage of them be channeled through for the use of local governments."[11] His proposal was clearly unappealing to Democrats on Capitol Hill: no hearings were held on it in 1969 or 1970.

In 1970, pressure for federal revenue sharing continued to be applied by state and local government officials who were destined to be the principal beneficiaries of the program. Members of the intergovernmental lobby, namely organizations representing state and local officials, wanted federal revenues without federal control; but they disagreed with one another over how much control states should have over the funds.[12]

President Nixon revived the administration's revenue sharing proposal in 1971, introducing it along with several other proposals to establish a New Federalism. The general revenue sharing part of the New Federalism package was much larger than the original Nixon bill. It proposed $5 billion for the first year and fixed the program to 1.3 percent of total taxable personal income, allowing it to grow with the national economy. To meet objections of local officials it proposed sharing 50 percent of the total pie with local governments, compared to the 27 percent they would have received under the 1969 bill.[13]

Hearings on the administration's proposal were finally held by the House Ways and Means Committee in 1971, but its chairman, Wilbur Mills, announced that he intended to kill the revenue sharing idea. At opening sessions of the hearings, Chairman Mills referred to revenue sharing as "the most dangerous proposal that has ever been developed. . . ." But under intense pressure from state and local officials, including Democratic mayors and governors, he reversed his position, announcing that revenue sharing would be acceptable if it met the "truly acute, immediate problems," of some cities and states.[14]

The bill produced by the Ways and Means Committee was the Intergovernmental Fiscal Coordination Act. It proposed an allocation of $5.3 billion over five years, thus matching the administration's figure; but it differed from the Nixon bill in several significant respects. In contrast to the administration-proposed one-to-one state/local split, the Ways and Means Committee's bill allocated one-third of the funds to the states and two-thirds to local governments. Instead of indexing revenue sharing to taxable income, the bill was funded through fixed appropriations and included language encouraging the enactment of state and local income taxes. Finally, while the administration's bill placed no substantive restrictions on shared revenues, the bill of the Mills Committee prohibited their use for matching grants to obtain other federal funds and limited shared revenues to "priority expenditure" categories—public safety, environment, and transportation—and a few capital investments. Over liberal objections that the bill abdicated federal responsibility, conservative objections to the usage restrictions, and outcries from various quarters that the bill should not bypass the normal appropriations process, the House approved the bill.

Late in June of 1972 the Senate Finance Committee took up consideration of revenue sharing. By this time the administration had decided to support the House-passed legislation while raising objections to the priority expenditure limitations and income tax incentives. The Senate dealt with the administration's objections by deleting the provisions that the administration found objectionable. The Senate also proposed a formula which would favor states with lower per capita incomes.

Conference committee meetings to reconcile House and Senate bills were held in late 1972. The conferees removed one of the largest obstacles to enactment by adopting *both* the House and Senate allocation formulas: state and local governments would select the formula providing them with the most funds. The conferees also broadened the areas of government activity included on the priority expenditure list, required planned and actual use reports from all grant recipients, and inserted various procedural restrictions, including prohibitions against discrimination.

Under the law signed by President Nixon in October 1972, nearly all general purpose local governments and all states are entitled to funding. Eighty percent of the 39,000 local governments that are eligible for GRS have populations of less than 2,500.[15] The allocations are first calculated for each state, using either the House or Senate formula, and then suballocated to cities, counties, and townships within the states.[16] Grants are automatically distributed by the Office of Revenue Sharing of the U.S. Department of the Treasury without any applications from subnational governments. Because the law passed in late 1972, allocations for that year were made retroactively. Consequently within about six months state and local governments received a 1.5-year allocation. Table 2-1 gives the yearly allocations for GRS from 1972 to 1980.

Table 2-1
Entitlement Periods and Funding for General Revenue Sharing, 1972-1980
(in billions of dollars)

Entitlement Periods	Amounts
January 1 to June 30, 1972	2.7
July 1 to December 31, 1972	2.7
January 1 to June 30, 1973	3.0
July 1, 1973 to June 30, 1974	6.1
July 1, 1974 to June 30, 1975	6.2
July 1, 1975 to June 30, 1976	6.4
July 1, 1976 to December 31, 1976	3.3
January 1 to September 30, 1977	5.0
October 1, 1977 to September 30, 1978	6.8
October 1, 1978 to September 30, 1979	6.9
October 1, 1979 to September 30, 1980	6.9

Source: U.S., Department of the Treasury, Office of Revenue Sharing, *Sixth Annual Report,* March 1, 1979 (Washington, D.C.: Government Printing Office), p. 15.

Graham Watt, director of the Office of Revenue Sharing, characterized General Revenue Sharing as "a simple, no-strings program, which is both extremely complicated and has important strings."[17] According to one analyst, the law is in the ambivalent position of being "neither . . . federal aid to achieve broadly defined, overriding national objectives, nor pure revenue sharing designed to give all state and local governments complete discretion on how to use the money."[18] General Revenue Sharing authorizes over $30 billion to state and local governments for use on a wide range of governmental needs and services and for general tax abatement; however, the law also contains important financial, policy, and constitutional strings that prescribe the way in which funds may be used, and thus asserts, though weakly, national goals.[19]

All levels of government are required to spend GRS funds in accordance with applicable state and local laws governing the use of locally raised funds. Grant recipients must also submit reports on planned and actual uses of funds to the Office of Revenue Sharing and publish them in local newspapers. Cities, counties, and townships must certify that they have spent their shared revenues only in the priority expenditure categories listed in the law. Funds may also be used to stabilize or reduce state and local taxes, but they may not be used as the state or local share for federal matching grants. Individuals employed in construction projects funded 25 percent or more by GRS funds must be paid at prevailing wages under the provisions of the Davis-Bacon Act of 1931. Projects that are funded in whole or in part by GRS may not discriminate against people in groups named in the law.

Expressing concern that once GRS was enacted it would continue forever, Congressman George Mahon, chairman of the House Appropriations Committee, observed: "The passage of the revenue sharing bill will organize and galvanize the most powerful lobby group this country has ever known."[20] Indeed, shortly after GRS's passage through Congress in 1972, state and local government organizations began the drive to have it reenacted. The second time around they wanted Congress to eliminate restrictions on the use of funds and authorize a permanent program.

But GRS had also attracted a number of critics who sought changes in the shape of the law. Various civil rights groups and some congressmen attacked state and local governments for failing to address the nation's poorest citizens, using the funds in a discriminatory manner, and excluding citizens from the budgetary process.[21] These groups turned their attention to strengthening the civil rights clause in the law and mandating citizen participation.

Opponents of the 1972 version of GRS found significant support from Congressman Jack Brooks, chairman of the House Government Operations Committee, where jurisdiction for the law had been transferred from the

Ways and Means Committee. But state and local officials and others who advocated removal of the remaining restrictions on the use of GRS funds were supported by the Ford administration, by members of the Subcommittee on Intergovernmental Relations of the House Government Operations Committee, and by members of the Senate Finance Committee.

After two years of intense debate and lobbying by both sides in the controversy, GRS was reauthorized in late 1976. Several important changes were effected, but the formula for dispersing funds was left basically intact. Extended for another 3.75 years, GRS would provide another $25 billion to state and local governments. But citizen participation was required for the first time. In addition to publication of planned uses and government budgets, the law mandated public hearings on the planned use of GRS funds. Recipients were also urged to involve senior citizens in the budget process. The law substantially strengthened civil rights provisions by expanding the list of groups covered by the nondiscrimination clause and by prohibiting discrimination in all activities of state and local government. State and local government activities would be exempt from the nondiscrimination requirement only where officials could present convincing evidence that GRS funds were not involved in supporting them. The law also established a more rapid timetable for processing civil rights complaints and authorized courts to award attorneys' fees to successful litigants in private discrimination suits. Financial accounting provisions were upgraded by requiring audits at least every three years in each jurisdiction.

Other changes weakened federal control. Congress removed the priority expenditure categories imposed on local governments in the 1972 law. Since the original law had contained no prohibition against substitution of federal funds for local funds and because GRS funds are extremely difficult to track once they reach a state or local government, most analysts found the 1972 restrictions without practical meaning. The antimatching stipulation in the original law was also stricken from the 1976 version of GRS.

Neither state and local officials nor the liberal critics got all they wanted in the 1976 revision of GRS. State and local officials won continued, substantial monetary support and fewer spending restrictions. Liberal critics succeeded in obtaining stronger civil rights language and mandatory citizen participation in GRS decision-making. Because the Congress continued to leave many aspects of the law vague, much discretion was handed over to federal administrators and to state and local officials for determining the precise shape of General Revenue Sharing.

Summary

In one sense the history of General Revenue Sharing is the story of a law in search of a clear purpose. Much of the debate over the statute concerned how Congress, national interest groups, state and local officials, and federal implementors defined its goals. State and local officials naturally preferred unrestricted aid for use on locally determined problems, and overall, the Congress supported this approach. But liberal members of Congress and civil rights groups viewed GRS as a vehicle for promoting other national goals. To these people, GRS represented an irresistible opportunity for influencing state and local governments to assist minority and low-income residents. Their efforts moved one official of the National Association of Counties to complain, "This is supposed to be the State and Local Fiscal Assistance Act. . . . It's not the 'Citizen Participation and Civil Rights Act of 1976.' "[22] The remainder of this chapter assesses how the law was implemented and what goals were given emphasis by federal, state, and local actors.

Implementing General Revenue Sharing: What Happened and Why?

Because of the diverse purposes assigned to General Revenue Sharing by various groups, it has been analyzed from a variety of perspectives. Government agencies, interest groups, and independent observers have evaluated the impact of General Revenue Sharing on

state and local taxes,

fiscal imbalances among communities and states,

the role of elected officials in general purpose government,

citizen participation in the budgetary process,

government reform and modernization,

federal influence and oversight,

state and local program innovation and experimentation,

antipoverty programs and low-income people,

state and local government expenditures, and

discrimination in employment and service distribution.

As one observer remarked, "Few programs in recent years have been advocated as a remedy for so many diverse and conflicting ills as Revenue Sharing."[23]

Since GRS constitutes only 2.6 percent of total state budgetary resources and only 3.4 percent of local resources and because the funds were intended as general assistance, it is reasonable to ask how all these expectations could be attached to GRS.[24] As Deil Wright reminds us, however, "It is unrealistic to compare the states' $2 billion share of GRS with the total tax or general revenues of state governments."[25] General Revenue Sharing funds are relatively unrestricted, whereas most state and locally raised revenues and other federal funds carry many conditions with them. Because GRS may be viewed by state and local officials as "free money," it may be an important catalyst for change in their priorities or approaches to decision-making. Moreover, other potentially important national goals were attached along with the more straightforward goal of general aid. For instance, the nondiscrimination clause for women, minorities, the aged, and other groups extended federal constitutional protections into communities that had never received federal aid before. The nondiscrimination provision was probably the law's most controversial aspect, because it represented the legislation's clearest attempt to influence state and local behavior.[26]

The analysis presented here examines the impact of GRS on the local budgetary process and its impact on government finances and expenditures. Because General Revenue Sharing is less a program than simply more money, evaluating its implementation is very difficult. Consequently, my analysis describes and explains changes brought about by GRS. No attempt is made to address the totality of state and local government decision-making or fiscal policy, nor are all the potential effects of GRS considered. The discussion of the federal government's role in GRS pays special attention to enforcement of the nondiscrimination provisions of the law. The question of who benefits from GRS is only briefly examined because there is insufficient evidence to warrant a lengthier discussion. Each section reviews the central policy issues, presents evidence on GRS's program performance, and provides explanations for the outcomes.

Who Governs? Elected Officials in the Budgetary Process; the Role of the Federal Government

There was little or no disagreement among participants in the legislative development of GRS that elected officials and administrative officers of state and local governments should be responsible for the allocation of shared revenues within their jurisdictions. There was considerable disagreement, however, about the degree of federal oversight that should be retained and the number of strings that should be attached to revenue sharing funds. According to the Advisory Commission on Intergovernmental Relations:

> Congress introduced an element of ambiguity as to its intent. . . . On the one hand, Congress clearly designed the program to strengthen decentralized

decisionmaking. On the other hand, Congress included certain vestiges of Federal direction over the state and local use of the funds because of the belief by many legislators [in Congress] that they will be held accountable for the proper use of these Federal funds.[27]

Some members of Congress felt that accountability for the use of funds could be accomplished in part through the publication of GRS reports in local newspapers. During the Senate's consideration of the legislation in 1972, Senator Russell Long, chairman of the Senate Finance Committee, told his colleagues:

> The people of each community will be far better policemen on the expenditure of their money than any committee of Congress would be. . . . We will rely . . . heavily on the fact that [state and local governments] will inform their own people as to how they will use the money, both before and after it is spent.[28]

In contrast with the categorical grant programs of the 1960s, such as Community Action Programs or Model Cities, however, the original revenue sharing law specified no mandatory form of citizen participation.

Congress made federal government agencies responsible for calculating and distributing GRS checks and for overseeing several important procedural and programmatic strings. (The latter will be discussed in the following section.) Here, the analysis focuses on the role of the Office of Revenue Sharing in carrying out its general responsibilities and in enforcing the nondiscrimination clauses of the act. Grant recipients must assure the federal government that they will not discriminate in employment or the distribution of program funds, "under any program or activity funded in whole or in part with [GRS] funds" (Section 122 [a]).[29]

Elected Officials and Citizens in the Budgetary Process

Independent empirical analyses of General Revenue Sharing found that the new funds were usually allocated through normal patterns of budgetary decision-making.[30] Mayors, city managers, county executives, and governors and their key aides have traditionally dominated choices about their jurisdiction's budget and continue to do so. Summarizing the findings from a national survey of over 800 local governments conducted by analysts based at the Survey Research Center (SRC) of the University of Michigan, its authors observed, "General revenue sharing appears to have had relatively little impact on the decisionmaking process in American cities, as perceived by those who are involved in this process on a day-to-day basis."[31]

Although most analysts noted little change in the political process brought about by the law, some did observe that GRS made an impact, especially in its initial year. Noting that their observations applied to only one-fifth of the sixty-five jurisdictions in their study, analysts at the Brookings Institution said that in these cases the law was "associated with" a relatively more competitive political process in which interest groups gained more access to decisions over the budget.[32]

While analysts cited abundant evidence of citizen participation in the budgetary process, little of it could be attributed to General Revenue Sharing alone, because most communities already held public hearings on their budgets. According to the Survey Research Center, two-thirds of all municipalities and 82 percent of all counties in their sample held at least one budgetary hearing prior to GRS. The largest counties and cities held hearings in all but 7 percent of the 800 communities. Some additional interest in the budgetary process was perceived by local officials due to general revenue sharing, however. Fifteen percent of the municipal executives, 31 percent of the county officials, and nearly half of the officials in cities over 300,000 suggested that GRS had increased public interest in budgetary matters.[33]

Most observers found that citizen participation in the allocation of GRS funds peaked in the first year when the first and largest single amount of money came to the jurisdictions. Since the first GRS checks frequently arrived in mid-year, and not in conjunction with the normal budgetary planning cycle, many communities scheduled special hearings on the allocation of revenue sharing monies.[34] The initially increased opportunities for citizen input declined in the second year, as GRS funds were integrated into the normal budgetary process.[35]

Increased influence by citizens' groups in the budgetary process and the allotment of GRS funds was occasionally achieved.[36] For example, the Brookings Institution study of sixty-five cities, counties, townships, and states attributed substantial influence to interest groups in nine jusidictions.[37] The National Clearinghouse on Revenue Sharing, an independent group established to monitor GRS and press for changes in the law, claimed that citizens' groups made an important impact on GRS budgets in ten of the sixty communities it investigated.[38] Although a great variety of groups participated in the budgetary process, social service agencies, senior citizens, and minorities tended to be most prominent in GRS decision-making, especially in the larger cities.[39]

The Federal Role

The Department of the Treasury's Office of Revenue Sharing (ORS) was the principal federal agency responsible for overseeing GRS. Involved to a lesser extent were the General Accounting Office, the Department of Justice, and the Department of Labor.

The Office of Revenue Sharing consistently took a low-key and non-interventionist posture in the initial years of GRS, concentrating its activities on assembling data for program allocations and collating the planned and actual use reports of state and local governments. The agency acted efficiently and effectively in carrying out these chores.[40]

Though the law's provisions would have permitted ORS to be more aggressive, its personnel displayed fealty to the philosophy of the New Federalism: they felt ORS should facilitate decentralization and not intervene in the decisions of state and local governments.[41] One result of ORS's general attitude was the decision to rely on complaints from citizens about the use of funds and adherence to GRS's provisions rather than build the capability to conduct compliance reviews in the field.[42] For example, in the initial years of GRS, ORS employed only nineteen staff members in its compliance unit, two of whom were assigned to civil rights enforcement.[43]

Independent analysts and civil rights organizations charged that ORS did not aggressively enforce the civil rights provision of the law. One review of ORS's performance found that of the 148 alleged violations of the non-discrimination clause brought to the attention of ORS, only fifteen led to a finding of noncompliance. Sanctions were applied in only two cases, one at the order of a federal court.[44] This same study accused ORS of failure to promote compliance through clear standards, failure to identify violations, and unwillingness to act promptly when violations were discovered.[45] Finding ORS's enforcement efforts "fundamentally inadequate," the U.S. Civil Rights Commission attacked the office for being "complacent in living up to [the] civil rights mandate."[46]

ORS responded to such criticisms by pointing out that it relied on other federal, state, and local agencies to handle civil rights complaints; that voluntary compliance was a more effective method of achieving results when allegations of discrimination were made; and that it could "not cut off funds to governments suspected of violating the civil rights provision, because the ORS does not believe the law gives it this power."[47]

There is evidence suggesting that ORS responded to the criticism by members of Congress and civil rights organizations by issuing stronger regulations and more detailed guides on how local governments could comply with the law.[48] But the major reorientation of ORS's enforcement effort was brought about by the 1976 reauthorization of GRS—a law that greatly expanded the nondiscrimination clause and set out specific timetables for agency action. Simultaneously, new senior personnel in the Department of the Treasury and ORS were ushered in by the election of Jimmy Carter to the presidency. For the first time, in 1977, ORS personnel conducted reviews in communities instead of waiting for citizen complaints, and the compliance staff was expanded to forty.[49]

Table 2-2
Status of Civil Rights Complaints Handled by the Office of Revenue Sharing, 1972-1978

Year	Received	Determination/ Finding	Closed	Carried Over
1972	2	0	0	2
1973	27	1	2	27
1974	75	14	26	76
1975	213	8	29	260
1976	229	7	71	418
1977	276	125	142	552
1978	306	156	184	674
Totals	1,128	311	454	

Source: U.S., Department of the Treasury, Office of Revenue Sharing, *Sixth Annual Report,* March 1, 1979 (Washington, D.C.: Government Printing Office), p. 2.

Evidence of stepped-up civil rights enforcement is presented in table 2-2, which is reproduced from the Sixth Annual Report of the Office of Revenue Sharing. The central change worth noting is the vastly increased number of cases listed in the "determinations and findings" and the "closed" categories in 1977 and 1978. ORS has sharply improved its administrative procedures for dealing with discrimination complaints. Greater numbers of complaints have been investigated and resolved during 1977 and 1978 than before. Though the data do not necessarily prove that the civil rights cases have been resolved satisfactorily, they do suggest an expanded commitment by ORS.

Explaining Who Governs: The Model Applied

The role of elected officials and political executives in budget decisions was basically unaffected by the advent of General Revenue Sharing funds. In a few instances the political process became more competitive and conflict among groups increased as they fought over the allocation of "new" money; but in many communities the funds were allocated before the law passed Congress, and there was nothing to struggle over. Citizen participation in local budgetary processes has always been limited, even though most communities hold public hearings on their budgets. General Revenue Sharing did not seem to have much impact on that fundamental relationship, either, but a few more citizens got involved in the initial years; after that, participation probably receded to pre-GRS levels. The Office of Revenue Sharing perceived its role as a facilitator of decentralization rather than an "avenging angel" for civil rights advocates.[50] ORS's role escalated and became more assertive during the years of the program, but it still would not be considered highly intrusive.

Policy Standards and Resources. The statute clearly established the authority of state and local officials to make GRS decisions without federal intervention, but it was not very important in shaping the specific budget process followed by those officials. Nevertheless, several features of the policy and its resources help account for patterns of governance.

1. GRS was not designed to reorder local budgetary decision-making, but some in Congress thought that the public reporting provisions would insure an opportunity for participation and provide citizens enough information to hold elected officials accountable for GRS uses. But just about everyone who has studied the planned and actual use reports has concluded that they mask the net impact of GRS funds—a point elaborated on in the section describing fiscal effects. The reports probably misled those people who did happen to read them and probably had little influence on the local political process.[51]

2. The policy also contradicts itself on the issue of stimulating public knowledge of the budgetary process. The law encourages state and local governments to merge GRS funds into their regular budgets, thus reducing the likelihood that GRS will attract public attention. But the statute also suggests that local officials might want to afford GRS special or separate treatment because of the use reports and the other procedural requirements.[52] In short, the law does not clearly indicate whether state and local officials should treat GRS as a new program or simply as more money.[53]

3. Where increased attention to budgetary politics and alterations in patterns of decision-making occurred, observers frequently attributed the changes to the fact that GRS funds arrived in communities in the middle of their fiscal years, outside the normal budgeting cycle.[54] For example, the Brookings Institution analysts concluded that the odd timing of GRS's arrival and the bunching of large amounts of funds in a short period of time were the principal explanations for the initial increase in public participation.[55] The subsequent decline in citizen participation may have come about because governments incorporated GRS into their normal budget routines after the first year. The 1976 reauthorization may reverse this trend because it mandates hearings on the budget that highlight the relationship of GRS funds to regular budget items.

4. Finally, the policy established contradictory mandates for the federal government. On the one hand, it clearly fosters decentralization by avoiding elaborate application requirements and performance evaluations. On the other hand, it includes the potential for federal intervention through such areas as the nondiscrimination provision. ORS initially followed that part of the law and legislative history that suggested limited federal involvement. In later years

and especially after the 1976 reauthorization, ORS became more aggressive, in part because the Congress was less ambiguous in its intent.

The National Policy Environment. Elements of the national policy environment were essential in accounting for the federal government's role in GRS and had some impact on local patterns of governance.

1. The Office of Revenue Sharing was pressured by various national interest groups and some members of Congress to undertake vigorous enforcement of civil rights policy under GRS.[56] ORS also felt the influence of state and local officials and the Nixon administration calling for a hands-off approach. At least during the initial years of GRS, a majority in Congress preferred the laissez-faire role for ORS. Twice, in 1973 and 1974, Congress refused ORS's request for more compliance staff. Although the increased federal enforcement of civil rights under GRS coincided with the revision of the law in late 1976, the new leadership brought in by the Carter administration probably also stimulated ORS's renewed activity.

2. National interest groups also had a minimal impact on local decision-making. The coalition of civil rights and minority interest groups that pressed for vigorous federal oversight attempted to stimulate more citizen involvement and civil rights enforcement at the state and local levels. Their effect seems to have been slight,[57] but anecdotal evidence demonstrates that they galvanized at least a few local citizens' groups.[58]

The Local Policy Environment. Several aspects of the local policy environment help explain how GRS was handled in the local budgetary process.

1. Naturally, elected officials displayed an interest in GRS because it represented a new source of revenue, but not all officials viewed GRS in the same way. There were wide variations in the methods for allocating the funds. In some communities, elected officials made GRS decisions themselves; in others, citizen advisory panels doled out the money. Hence the general orientations of elected officials toward GRS helped determine whether GRS would be treated as a new program with a separate budgetary process and perhaps special citizen input.

By far the most important local condition affecting elected officials' attitudes about GRS was the degree of fiscal pressure evident in their jurisdictions. For example, Brookings researchers found that, in sixteen out of nineteen cases, chief executives and their staffs dominated budgetary processes where fiscal pressure was high. Legislative bodies and interest groups were more influential in cases where fiscal pressure was lower.[59] Jurisdictions facing higher fiscal pressures were also more likely to integrate shared revenue into their regular budgetary processes.[60]

Where local officials regarded shared revenue *as extra funds* GRS was more likely to be given special and usually more visible attention. While the objective needs of the jurisdiction influenced the orientations of local officials toward GRS, Brookings researchers noted that "local political conditions and attitudes . . . appear to have had more influence in effecting . . . [changes in the political process]."[61]

2. The impact of participation by citizens and interest groups was affected by the attitudes of local officials. Elected officials generally did not view enlarged roles for citizens in the budgetary process as an essential goal of the revenue sharing law. Less than one-fifth of city and county executives favored the formation of citizen advisory committees for General Revenue Sharing, according to the Survey Research Center poll.[62] And less than one-third of the senior administrative officials and elected leaders in Steven Waldhorn's study of ten large cities thought that citizen participation was an important aspect of General Revenue Sharing.[63]

The degree of citizen involvement in budgetary matters was also shaped by traditions established long before GRS funds were allocated. Public hearings on GRS were much more common in cities with populations of over 100,000, where budget hearings were already a regular feature of the political process.[64] What this may suggest is that officials in larger, more complex political environments found it necessary to incorporate more citizen participation into budget decisions and the use of GRS.

Summary

Patterns of governance for General Revenue Sharing were determined principally by the local policy environment, especially the atttitudes of local officials and the fiscal conditions of the community or state. The national policy environment had a very modest effect on local decisions, but did influence the federal role in monitoring GRS's various strings. The law's policy standards and resources permitted state and local officials to establish preferred governance approaches.

What Are the Fiscal and Programmatic Effects of General Revenue Sharing?

General Revenue Sharing provided general assistance to state and local governments to use, within broad guidelines, on public services or tax relief. The prevailing rhetoric at the time of its enactment called for increased freedom of choice for state and local officials. President Nixon expressed this view when he signed the State and Local Fiscal Assistance Act:

> Under this program, instead of spending so much time trying to please distant bureaucrats in Washington . . . officials can concentrate on pleasing the people. . . . When we say no strings we mean no strings.[65]

But those who were less enthusiastic about the revenue sharing approach wanted to insure accountability for the use of GRS both to the federal government and to residents of state and local political jurisdictions. They felt that the federal government must be able to trace the use of shared revenues.

Liberal critics, in particular, voiced concern over the impact that GRS might have on the disadvantaged members of the communities, the poor and minorities. Testifying at an October 1973 hearing organized by the Advisory Commission on Intergovernmental Relations, then Governor Jimmy Carter of Georgia stated the classic liberal argument against revenue sharing as opposed to other forms of federal aid:

> Categorical grants have been designed as contracts between the Federal government and the state or local government with a clearly understood, predictable sharing responsibility for meeting needs that were identified to be unmet by state and local programs. . . . When these funds are taken away from the poor and put into general revenue sharing or block grants, even the most enlightened legislature is not going to take these funds and put them back exclusively into programs that benefit the poor. They are going to spread them uniformly among all the citizens.[66]

Although the legislation made no mention of serving low-income groups, the extent to which GRS benefited the poor was frequently raised by interest groups and produced controversy during the 1976 reauthorization debate.[67]

GRS neither removes all federal goals and oversight nor asserts clear national standards, but several potentially important restrictions were placed on the general assistance money. State and local governments were prohibited from applying revenue sharing funds as their share of a federal matching grant, from discriminating in employment or the distribution of services, and from shortchanging workers on construction projects who must be paid the prevailing local wage under the Davis-Bacon Act.

State governments could allocate their shared revenue for any public service or capital projects authorized by their own laws. Local governments could also spend GRS on legally authorized capital projects, but the law ordered them to place GRS dollars within eight priority expenditure categories. According to one observer, the priority expenditure stipulation was "included in the 1972 Act as a concession (or sop) to sentiment favoring some control or direction by Congress over the use of the funds."[68] Overall the law's restrictions did not seriously undermine the goal of giving state and local governments broad discretion over the application of federal shared revenues.

Although General Revenue Sharing has been evaluated extensively by government agencies, research institutes, university-based analysts, and interest groups, evidence necessary to assess thoroughly its fiscal and programmatic effects is less than satisfactory. It is difficult to track GRS funds because of their "fungibility": once GRS funds are entered in the general accounts of state and local governments they become indistinguishable from other funds.[69] Reaching a pessimistic conclusion on the question of assessing GRS usage, the Advisory Commission on Intergovernmental Relations said:

> It is virtually impossible to determine on an aggregate basis how revenue sharing funds have been spent. As revenue sharing becomes a recurring item in state and local budgets, its novelty, and hence its visibility will diminish. . . . It remains questionable whether it will ever be possible to fully assess the ultimate impact of revenue sharing on state and local expenditure decisions and priorities.[70]

Other analysts reached similar conclusions after exhaustive studies of shared revenues.[71]

The legislation required local governments to prepare planned and actual use reports, but because of the fungibility of funds these have proven inadequate to reveal the true fiscal and programmatic effects of GRS.[72] The use reports require that local officials designate the accounts into which shared revenues are placed, but, according to the U.S. General Accounting Office, "Accounting designations of the uses of revenue sharing are illusory and should not be interpreted to indicate increased or improved services in the functions or activities that have been designated."[73] Congressman Henry Reuss made the same point more bluntly: "The Actual Use reports are an exercise in creative paper work, and no more."[74]

While reliance on the ofificial GRS use reports would be foolhardy, there are several useful alternative sources of information from major studies of the program. Analysts have employed careful observation and intensive case studies,[75] surveys of state and local executives and finance officers,[76] and statistical analyses of financial time series data in order to construct estimates of the effects of GRS.[77] The advantage of the intensive field research is that it allows a skilled observer to employ a variety of data sources and interviews and to pursue answers for questions that are particularly complex. The principal disadvantage of this approach is that the number of jurisdictions examined is never large enough to be representative of all jurisdictions. The survey approach to estimating GRS uses can overcome the problem of representativeness by employing an appropriate sampling strategy, but the obvious disadvantage is that the full range of respondents in a community and other data sources cannot be investigated in depth. The statistical modeling techniques are appealing, but they have been conducted in only a very small sample of jurisdictions.[78]

Since both the survey approach and the case study method have strengths and weaknesses, data displaying the results of both kinds of analysis will be exhibited. Moreover, wherever possible, patterns of estimated GRS usage will be compared with typical allocations of state and local government revenues, using data from the Census of Governments conducted by the U.S. Census Bureau.

Fiscal Effects of General Revenue Sharing

Estimates of the fiscal effects of General Revenue Sharing derived from the Survey Research Center's report on several hundred local governments are presented in the top part of table 2-3. Basically the figures are constructed from answers to a sequence of questions posed to finance officers about what their jurisdictions would have done in the way of local expenditures, borrowing, and taxing in the absence of GRS. A series of assumptions about how funds would be allocated is then made to translate the qualitative responses into quantitative estimates.[79]

In general, the SRC estimates indicate that in fiscal year 1974, GRS's major fiscal impact was felt in maintaining and increasing capital expenditures; nearly one-third of the funds were used for operating expenditures; and GRS had only a limited impact on local taxes. The tax effect of GRS increased significantly in the second year of the program.

These patterns differ widely according to the sizes of local governmental jurisdictions. Cities over 300,000 used much larger proportions of shared revenues for operating expenditures; smaller communities put much more of their GRS funds into capital projects. Tax relief was the most preferred use of GRS funds in cities with populations of 100,000 to 299,999 and became much more prominent in the largest cities, those over 300,000, in fiscal year 1975.

Data from the Brookings Institution's research in sixty-five jurisdictions appear on the bottom half of table 2-3. Their methodology was entirely different from that of the SRC. Instead of surveying a large number of officials, they relied on the findings of experienced field researchers who studied GRS in depth in their communities. Although it is the most comprehensive of the case study approaches, Brookings' group of jurisdictions is much smaller than the SRC sample and was not intended as a representative sample of all governments in the United States.

The overall data show that GRS served as a vehicle for tax reduction or stabilization during the initial period. Lesser amounts of GRS funds were applied to mount capital projects or to maintain or expand existing programs. The SRC analysts argue, however, that a more appropriate comparison of the Brookings findings with the SRC's estimates can be made by deleting New York City's use of GRS from the Brookings data. Since the data are weighted means, the extraordinarily large amount of New York City's GRS allocation (approximately 40 percent of the total Brookings group) has a significant impact on the averages. As shown in the bottom row of table 2-3, "The estimated 40 percent of revenue-sharing funds used for tax stabilization turns out to be more like 20 percent if one simply excludes New York City from the calculation."[80] While these comparisons are at best suggestive, they do indicate that, when the New York City adjustment is made, the Brookings results are not much different from the SRC estimates of fiscal effect.

In contrast with the manner in which local governments normally allocate their funds, GRS was concentrated much more heavily on capital outlays in counties, townships, and municipalities. For example, between 1970 and 1972, local governments used about 15 percent of their resources on capital outlays, according to Census Bureau reports.[81] Both the SRC and Brookings studies estimate GRS allocations for capital projects at a much higher level, closer to 40 percent.

An alternative method of examining the impact of GRS, based on some different Brookings Institution data, is presented in table 2-4. In this table the percentages are unweighted means, derived by averaging the percentages of each community in their sample: results for the analysis of New York City are treated the same as those for Cottage Grove, Oregon, one of the smaller communities in their study. This method of presentation may be thought of as a way to represent decisions on how shared revenues were used rather than a measure that accounts for dollar allocations.[82] These data also have the additional advantages of allowing more detailed breakdowns of fiscal effects and comparisons of state governments with local governments.

Local governments utilized roughly equal proportions of GRS funds in the new spending category (capital projects and government services) and the substitution category (program maintenance and tax abatement). In contrast, state governments used larger amounts of shared revenues in the substitution category of fiscal effects. Local governments reduced the amount of GRS funds for new capital projects between the first round (up to July 1973) and the second round (up to July 1974) of the Brookings research. Most of the increases occurred in the tax stabilization and program maintenance categories. State governments consistently spent about one-fifth of their GRS funds on capital expenditures, but increased GRS allocations for tax relief in the second period. According to the analysts at Brookings, larger jurisdictions placed less of their GRS resources into capital projects than did smaller towns and counties, whereas cities more commonly used their GRS money to avert program cutbacks.[83]

Table 2-3
Estimated Fiscal Effects of General Revenue Sharing on State and Local Governments,
Fiscal Years 1974 and 1975
(in percent)

Type of Unit	Number of Cases	Fiscal Impact Category				
		Maintained or Increased Operating Expenditures	Maintained or Increased Capital Expenditures	Stabilized or Reduced Local Taxes	Other	Total Revenue Sharing Allocation
Survey Research Center Estimates[a]						
Municipalities, fiscal year 1974						
Over 300,000	27	68.5	13.1	11.1	7.3	100.0
100,000-299,000	40	28.4	27.0	42.1	2.4	100.0
100-99,999	512	12.5	54.8	17.8	15.0	100.0
Townships	72	16.1	45.4	11.4	27.0	100.0
Counties	142	21.9	49.0	13.9	15.3	100.0
Grand Total	793	28.7	41.8	16.6	13.0	100.0
Municipalities, fiscal year 1975						
Over 300,000	27	51.9	13.4	34.1	0.5	100.0
100,000-299,000	40	30.3	33.7	37.6	-0.2	100.0
100-99,999	512	18.9	50.9	22.1	8.1	100.0
Townships	72	21.3	42.7	12.2	23.8	100.0
Counties	142	21.9	42.7	21.5	14.0	100.0
Grand total	793	27.5	38.8	25.0	8.7	100.0

Brookings Institution Estimates,[b] up to July 1, 1973					
States and local governments	65	18	27	40	15	100
(Excluding New York City)[c]	64	29	44	22	5	100

[a]F. Thomas Juster, ed., *The Economic and Political Impact of General Revenue Sharing* (Washington, D.C.: Government Printing Office, 1976), table 2-6, p. 27. Surveys of Finance Officers.

[b]Calculated from data in Richard P. Nathan et al., *Monitoring Revenue Sharing* (Washington, D.C.: The Brookings Institution, 1975), table 8-3, p. 199. Field Research associates' estimates.

[c]Calculated from data in F. Thomas Juster, table 2-7, p. 29.

Programmatic Effects of General
Revenue Sharing

The SRC's survey of local officials produced estimates of the programmatic or functional categories in which shared revenues were used. They are displayed in table 2-5. Again these estimates are based on responses to the SRC survey and assumptions about the allocation of GRS among functional categories.[84]

In general, public safety received the largest share of resources at the local level, followed by public transportation, environmental protection, and so-called amenities, such as recreation and libraries. Education and social service programs were given very small amounts of GRS funds. There was little change during the two years of the SRC study.

Substantial differences on the programmatic uses of GRS were found among communities of different sizes. For example, counties spent more GRS money than municipalities did on social services, but considerably less on environmental protection, recreation, and libraries. Smaller cities and townships were much more likely than larger communities to put their GRS allocation into public transportation.

Table 2-6 provides a comparison of GRS's program uses with the normal expenditures of local governments. The principal departures from typical patterns are in the education and amenities categories. Local governments allocated about three times as much for education under typical spending patterns than they did under General Revenue Sharing, according to the SRC estimates. They also used a much higher percentage than normal of their GRS funds for recreation, libraries and other amenities.

Useful evidence on the programmatic effects of shared revenues in the states is available from a survey of state agency heads conducted by Deil Wright and associates. Their estimates, reproduced in table 2-7, show that states put the majority of their GRS money into educational programs. Smaller but significant amounts went to criminal justice and economic development categories. Very low amounts were spent on social services and health. According to Wright the estimated use of General Revenue Sharing "departs radically from the typical aggregate expenditure pattern of the states. In 1974, for example, the states' major direct expenditures were education, 27 percent; welfare, 21 percent; highways, 17 percent; and health/hospitals, 10 percent."[85]

An alternative method for calculating the programmatic effects of GRS was employed by field associates of the Brookings Institution, who categorized the use of GRS into the nine functional areas displayed in table 2-8. These data should *not* be compared with the SRC or Wright survey estimates, because they are not a representative sample and account for only a portion of GRS funds. States used the largest proportions of their GRS

Table 2-4
Estimated Fiscal Effects of General Revenue Sharing on State and
Local Governments, Derived from the Brookings Institution Study
(unweighted means, in percent)

Net Fiscal Effect	Round 1[a]	Round 2[b]	Cumulative
Local Governments[c]			
New spending[d]	56.2	45.9	51.8
New capital	45.2	34.5	41.4
Expanded operations	10.5	10.6	9.6
Increased pay and benefits	0.5	0.8	0.8
Substitutions	43.9	52.4	47.0
Program maintenance	12.8	14.6	13.5
Restoration of federal aid	0.4	1.1	0.8
Tax reduction	3.8	5.0	4.4
Tax stabilization	14.1	18.3	15.3
Avoidance of borrowing	9.6	7.7	8.8
Increased fund balance	2.8	3.4	3.0
Substitution not categorized	0.4	2.3	1.2
Balance of allocation[e]	0.1	1.6	1.2
State Governments			
New spending	35.7	39.6	37.3
New capital	21.1	21.0	21.0
Expanded operations	12.1	13.2	13.8
Increased pay and benefits	0.0	5.4	1.2
New spending not categorized	2.5	0.0	1.3
Substitutions	64.3	58.2	62.5
Program maintenance	15.3	0.0	6.7
Restoration of federal aid	3.0	13.3	7.8
Tax reduction	13.2	12.0	12.2
Tax stabilization	0.0	12.5	7.6
Avoidance of borrowing	3.3	2.5	4.0
Increased fund balance	4.5	5.4	4.6
Substitution not categorized	25.0	12.5	19.6
Balance of allocation[e]	0.0	2.4	0.1

Source: Richard P. Nathan, Charles Adams, Jr., and associates, *Revenue Sharing: The Second Round* (Washington, D.C.: The Brookings Institution, 1977), p. 31. Reprinted with permission. Copyright © by the Brookings Institution.

[a]Allocations up to July 1, 1973.

[b]Allocations up to June 30, 1974.

[c]In round 1, three local governments allocated no revenue sharing funds; in round 2, one local government made no allocation.

[d]Figures may not add to totals because of rounding. Cumulative figures do not coincide with a simple averaging over the first- and second-round figures because of differences within the jurisdictions in the amounts allocated in the two rounds.

[e]Net effect not categorized as between new spending and substitution.

funds in public transportation, environmental protection, and education; cities put GRS funds into public safety, transportation, environmental protection, and recreation. Townships targeted their GRS funds on transporta-

Table 2-5

Estimated Programmatic Effect of General Revenue Sharing on Local Governments, Derived from the Survey Research Center Study, for Fiscal Years 1974 and 1975

(percent of GRS allocated to each category)

Government Type and Size Class	Public Safety	Environment	Land Use	Transportation	Amenities	Education	Health	Social Service	Admin. & Finance	Other	Residual	Total
						Fiscal Year 1974						
Municipalities												
300,000 and over	15.1	13.8	1.2	9.6	19.9	6.2	11.6	0.2	4.9	4.3	13.2	100.0
100,000-299,999	31.6	8.7	6.2	5.5	18.7	2.2	7.1	2.7	6.3	1.5	9.3	100.0
25,000-99,999	18.4	19.1	3.0	19.3	20.9	2.4	3.2	1.5	8.1	1.8	2.3	100.0
10,000-24,999	26.2	21.3	0.4	25.8	8.1	2.0	0.3	0.3	4.6	0.8	10.2	100.0
2,500-9,999	25.1	29.2	3.0	26.1	8.2	0.4	0.2	0.1	1.4	0.8	5.5	100.0
Less than 2,500	16.9	14.9	1.0	26.6	18.9	0.2	0.3	0.2	8.2	2.6	10.1	100.0
Townships, 9000 and over	21.7	7.3	10.1	18.9	12.4	1.7	6.5	8.2	6.5	1.1	5.6	100.0
Townships, less than 9000	5.4	11.3	0.7	52.7	9.2	0.2	–	–	2.1	10.4	8.0	100.0
Counties												
500,000 and over	19.6	1.2	4.3	5.7	7.6	3.8	7.4	9.1	5.5	1.2	34.3	100.0
100,000-499,999	16.9	4.1	3.8	18.6	7.8	3.7	9.4	5.7	9.5	1.6	18.7	100.0
Less than 100,000	29.9	0.9	6.6	18.7	12.5	5.7	9.1	2.8	8.4	1.7	3.6	100.0
All	20.8	9.7	4.2	16.6	14.4	3.7	6.8	3.8	6.7	2.2	11.0	100.0

Fiscal Year 1975

Government Type and Size Class	Public Safety	Environment	Land Use	Transportation	Amenities	Education	Health	Social Service	Admin. & Finance	Other	Residual	Total
Municipalities												
300,000 and over	18.4	14.8	1.2	9.6	16.0	6.2	12.5	0.1	3.7	4.3	13.2	100.0
100,000-299,999	44.0	11.1	5.0	4.5	14.2	2.2	2.0	0.8	5.2	1.5	9.4	100.0
25,000-99,999	23.0	26.5	1.0	16.2	17.5	2.4	1.7	0.3	7.2	1.8	2.3	100.0
10,000-24,999	28.0	29.4	0.4	21.5	4.4	1.3	0.3	0.0	3.5	0.8	10.2	100.0
2,500-9,999	16.6	16.0	8.4	24.7	9.4	0.2	0.2	16.6	4.2	0.4	3.3	100.0
Less than 2,500	19.9	15.4	1.0	31.5	12.7	0.2	0.0	0.0	6.7	2.6	10.0	100.0
Townships, 9000 and over	29.2	31.2	0.3	22.4	4.5	1.4	0.6	—	3.7	1.1	5.6	100.0
Townships, less than 9000	20.5	15.8	0.9	32.7	13.4	—	—	—	6.8	1.4	8.0	100.0
Counties												
500,000 and over	20.0	0.5	1.8	15.7	5.9	3.4	7.8	3.8	5.5	0.8	34.7	100.0
100,000-499,999	23.4	1.7	2.0	18.4	6.9	5.4	9.8	5.0	6.9	1.7	18.6	100.0
Less than 100,000	28.4	1.5	2.5	22.3	8.5	5.8	11.6	5.8	8.2	1.7	3.6	100.0
All	24.2	12.2	2.3	17.3	11.1	3.8	6.8	3.3	5.8	2.0	11.0	100.0

Source: F. Thomas Juster, ed., *The Economic and Political Impacts of General Revenue Sharing* (Washington, D.C.: Government Printing Office, 1976), table 3-3, p. 57 (for fiscal year 1974) and table 3-5, p. 58 (for fiscal year 1975).

Table 2-6
Local Government Budgets Typically Spent on Functional Categories by Size and Type of Government during Fiscal Year 1971
(in percent)

Local Government Type and Size Class	Total Expenditures (in millions of dollars)	Public Safety	Environmental Control	Land Use	Transportation	Amenities	Education	Health	Services	Financial	Other	Total
Municipalities												
300,000 and over	19,720.6	19.9	16.1	3.6	9.6	4.7	18.2	8.0	0.2	6.8	12.9	100
100,000-299,999	5,008.3	19.6	22.6	3.5	8.0	6.5	17.3	2.8	1.2	7.4	11.1	100
25,000-99,999	7,537.2	20.4	25.2	1.9	9.7	6.5	14.2	3.8	0.3	7.3	10.7	100
10,000-24,999	3,334.2	19.8	34.9	0.7	12.0	5.3	7.2	3.6	0.1	7.6	8.8	100
2,500-9,999	2,738.2	17.7	39.5	0.6	13.6	4.1	3.4	3.4	0.1	8.2	9.4	100
Less than 2,500	973.0	19.1	11.4	0.0	20.0	1.0	3.3	0.05	0.3	9.7	35.2	100
Counties	19,743.8	15.6	4.3	0.0	13.8	3.2	20.2	14.1	9.1	10.1	9.6	100
Total		18.4	15.9	1.8	11.4	4.5	16.7	8.5	3.3	8.2	11.0	100

Source: Data from the U.S. Census of Governments reported in F. Thomas Juster, ed., *The Economic and Political Impacts of General Revenue Sharing* (Washington, D.C.: Government Printing Office, 1976), table 3-7, p. 60.

Table 2-7
Estimated Programmatic Effect of General Revenue Sharing on State
Governments, Derived from a Survey of State Agency Heads, for
Fiscal Year 1974
(in percent)

Expenditure Category	Estimated Use
Education	51.4
Economic development	14.2
Criminal justice	11.6
Transportation	6.6
Health	4.4
Environment/energy	3.3
Natural resources	2.8
Social services	1.7
Other	4.0
Total	100.0

Source: Deil S. Wright et al., *Assessing the Impacts of General Revenue Sharing in the Fifty States: A Survey of State Administrators* (Chapel Hill: Institute for Research in the Social Sciences, University of North Carolina, 1975), table VI-2, p. VI-12. Reprinted with permission.

tion and environmental protection areas. Following the general pattern revealed by other estimates of GRS usage, the Brookings data show low expenditures on social services.

Who Benefits from General Revenue Sharing within Jurisdictions?

Most analysts of GRS reached conclusions similar to those reported by the National Science Foundation: "To estimate how much different segments of the population have benefited from the GRS program has proved to be extremely difficult, if not impossible."[86] Some observers, focusing on the low social service expenditures, concluded that General Revenue Sharing was shortchanging the poor.[87] But using the percentage of funds spent on social services as an indicator of the extent to which the disadvantaged benefited from GRS is an inadequate and inappropriate measure. Low-income groups benefit from other programs provided through or supported with General Revenue Sharing funds, including public transportation, and public safety particularly.[88] Moreover, when shared revenues help eliminate, stabilize, or reduce regressive taxes, such as sales taxes, benefits to low-income individuals may occur. Finally, even revenue sharing's severest critics found significant benefits for low-income residents in some communities.[89]

Unfortunately systematic evidence is scant, but the dominant impres-

Table 2-8
Estimated Programmatic Effect of General Revenue Sharing on
State and Local Governments, Derived from the Brookings
Institution Study
(unweighted means, in percent)

	Type of Government[a]			
Program	States (n = 7)	Counties (n = 21)	Cities (n = 27)	Townships (n = 6)
Public safety	2.7	8.4	16.6	2.2
Environmental protection	9.2	3.6	7.9	23.2
Public transportation	16.1	14.4	11.7	25.4
Health	6.4	3.4	1.2	0
Recreation	1.3	3.6	6.5	4.5
Library	1.3	2.5	0.9	0.5
Social services	2.5	3.3	3.3	0
Education	7.4	4.7	0	0
Other	3.8	10.9	5.8	13.8
Balance not allocated to a specific program	3.5	5.8	5.7	0
All programs[b]	54.2	60.6	59.8	69.6

Source: Richard P. Nathan, Charles Adams, Jr., and associates, *Revenue Sharing: The Second Round* (Washington, D.C.: The Brookings Institution, 1977), p. 68. Reprinted with permission. Copyright ©1977 by The Brookings Institution.

[a]Orlando, Florida, New York City, and the state of Illinois are excluded from the computations.

[b]This row is the total programmatic expenditures of GRS funds plus the amount not traced to specific program areas. It accounts for four of the Brookings net fiscal effect categories: new capital, new or expanded operations, program maintenance, and federal aid restoration.

sion given by national studies and government reports is that GRS, which was not designed as relief for the economically disadvantaged, has not been used for that purpose by most communities. For example, the Brookings field researchers found that shared revenues "provided significant benefits to the disadvantaged" in only seven of their sixty-five research sites.[90] An additional fifteen were judged to have afforded at least some assistance to low-income and minority residents through GRS.[91]

When all the reports are analyzed there is neither support for the case that GRS did not aid low-income people nor strong evidence that GRS provided substantial benefits to the poor in many communities. Consequently, most debates about who benefits from revenue sharing are really disagreements over how much the poor *should* benefit. There simply is not enough information to sustain a careful analysis, because GRS funds are so difficult to trace and because determining their impact on the poor is even harder.

Explaining the Fiscal and Programmatic Effects
of GRS: The Model Applied

General Revenue Sharing's fiscal effects varied with community size and over time. Large proportions of the funds were committed on capital expenditures, most prominently in smaller communities. Maintaining ongoing programs has commanded the second greatest share of GRS funds. Tax relief absorbed about 20 percent of shared revenues. Programmatic effects of GRS also varied across communities and departed significantly from typical spending patterns of state and local governments. Public safety, transportation, and environmental protection led functional uses of GRS at the local level. State governments put much larger amounts into education, often as part of aid packages for local governments. Sparse amounts of GRS funds were spent on social services. Little solid information was available about the impact of GRS on population subgroups within states, counties, cities, and townships. GRS has not been a boon to low-income people, nor have they been ignored by the program: poor people benefited both from various programmatic uses and through some tax relief efforts.

Policy Standards and Resources. Overall the statute was not very influential in determining the uses of GRS, but a few points about the effect of the policy standards and resources are worth noting.

1. The priority expenditure limitation on local governments had little effect on their decisions. Only 19 percent of the finance officers questioned in the Survey Research Center poll felt that direct expenditures of GRS funds would have been different without priority expenditure restrictions;[92] for some communities, however, the exclusion of education from the acceptable list pushed funds into less preferred areas of capital and operating expenditures.[93] The principal explanation for the unimpressive impact of the priority expenditure clause is that GRS funds are fungible. Local officials could place GRS funds in accounts covering the priority list—a list that was very broad to begin with—and then put the displaced state or local funds into functional areas where GRS use was forbidden.

2. The prohibition against matching federal grants with GRS funds had a greater influence on local choices. Over one-third of the finance officers in the SRC study indicated that their allocations would have been different without the antimatching standard; 30 percent said increases would have come in the category of social service expenditures.[94] The Brookings study reported that the antimatching provision influenced GRS decisions in eleven of its sixty-five study areas.[95] In short, the elimination of the priority expenditure and antimatching requirements in the 1976 legislation is likely to have very different effects. Striking the former will not make much dif-

ference; removal of the latter may cause some shifts and increase social service spending.

3. The relatively short duration of General Revenue Sharing and uncertainty over continued funding influenced some communties to put higher proportions of their GRS funds into capital projects and equipment than into programs representing longer range commitments for salaries or services to residents.[96]

4. Finally, the general structure of categorical and block grant aid from the federal government probably shaped GRS allocations by state and local governments. For instance, both the Comprehensive Employment and Training Act of 1973 and the Community Development Block Grant of 1974 offered local governments resources targeted at least partially to low- and moderate-income people. During the late 1970s these grants may have relieved pressure that local officials were getting from community groups and lessened demands for putting GRS into social services and community development programs. In addition, relatively high concentrations of funds in the transportation and safety categories may be partially explained by the fact that federal aid to state and local governments for these areas has been traditionally low.[97]

The National Policy Environment. Both by design and by choice the Office of Revenue Sharing made little impact on the decisions of state and local governments. ORS, committed to fostering decentralization, issued regulations and generally conducted its oversight of GRS in such a way as to give grant recipients maximum freedom. One analyst suggested, however, that ORS was more aggressive in carrying out the antimatching provision than the priority expenditure restrictions.[98] National interest groups, representing public employees, librarians, senior citizens, and minorities, attempted to galvanize their local affiliates to seek larger shares of the GRS pie, but they were not very successful.[99]

The Local Policy Environment. Several aspects of the local policy environment help account for the uses of GRS.

1. The *attitudes of local officials* about the proper scope and nature of governmental activities helped determine GRS expenditures and tax relief effects. For example, relatively low levels of social service spending may be explained by a belief held by many officials that such programs are not consistent with their jurisdiction's responsibilities. One group that was highly critical of the low expenditures on social service programs observed that *"it is clear that many city officials . . . continue to see their functions as narrowly traditional*, centering on public safety, roads, sanitation, and the like" (emphasis in original).[100] Sharp differences between state and local

levels and between governments of varying size may also be due to the widely divergent responsibilities exercised by different governmental jurisdictions, many of which are severely constrained by state and local laws.[101]

Although one would normally expect the past preferences and commitments of local officials to influence GRS (and they did to a large
extent),[102] the evidence presented above suggests some very interesting
departures from past practices. Much of this shift may be explained by the
factors discussed in the section on governance patterns. Many officials
viewed revenue sharing as an opportunity to break from their typical spending patterns. The relatively unrestricted nature of GRS probably led some
officials to apply GRS on capital projects which often require the approval
of bond issues by the public when revenues are raised locally. As one analyst
put it, state and local officials frequently viewed GRS as a "windfall," a
program for innovation and experimentation and for completing projects
that had previously been lower down their list of priorities.[103]

2. *Local fiscal conditions* and other measures of objective need also
played a major part in explaining the application of GRS funds and differences among communities. In general larger, fiscally hard-pressed cities
more often allotted larger proportions of their GRS funds to program
maintenance and tax relief than did smaller communities under light or no
fiscal strain.[104] Cities with lower per capita income spent more on social
services; those with higher per capita income spent more on capital expenditures.[105] Older, larger communities quickly absorbed revenue sharing funds
into their budgets to make ends meet, while smaller, less financially distressed jurisdictions placed their GRS funds in new programs or capital
projects. Finally, communities that spent more money on programs for low-
income people were experiencing less fiscal pressure than other communities.[106]

3. *Citizen participation* had some impact on shared revenue allocations, but it was not as important as the other factors in the local policy environment. David Caputo and Richard Cole report that cities holding public
hearings were less likely to allocate GRS funds to public safety agencies and
slightly more likely to provide social services for the poor and aged.[107] Cities
holding hearings were somewhat more prone to fund health and social service programs than those that did not, whereas counties holding GRS hearings allocated less for health and social services, according to the Survey
Research Center's analysis.[108] Not all of the active citizens desired more
social services, nor were "social action" groups important in many communities. Brookings found no significant activity from such groups in
thirty-nine of their sixty-five jurisdictions.[109] The central point about citizen
influence is that state and local officials determined whether citizens would
participate in GRS decisions and which ones they would listen to.[110]

Summary

The explanation of the fiscal and programmatic effects of GRS offers some insights into why GRS funds were used in ways that frequently differed from typical spending patterns in the states and communities. Policy standards and resources were not designed to be restrictive and they did not greatly influence GRS outcomes; however, both the short duration of the law, which probably stimulated higher spending on capital projects, and the antimatching provision, which apparently reduced social service spending, had noticable effects. The national policy environment had almost no influence over the use of General Revenue Sharing. Local policy environment factors were, as might be expected, the key determinants of GRS's effects. The fiscal condition of the jurisdiction guided GRS outcomes, as did the attitudes of local officials toward GRS and the scope of local government in general. Citizen groups had sporadic influence on GRS spending.

Notes

1. *Congressional Quarterly Almanac* 38 (1972):641.

2. New Orleans Mayor Moon Landrieu, as quoted in Joel Havemann, "Last-Minute Extension of Revenue Sharing Expected," *National Journal Reports* 7 (1975):1142.

3. Richard P. Nathan et al., *Monitoring Revenue Sharing* (Washington, D.C.: The Brookings Institution, 1975), pp. 3-4.

4. David A. Caputo and Richard L. Cole, *Urban Politics and Decentralization: The Case of General Revenue Sharing* (Lexington, Mass.: Lexington Books, D.C. Heath and Company, 1974), p. 17.

5. Ibid., p. 19.

6. Samuel H. Beer, "The Adoption of General Revenue Sharing: A Case Study in Public Sector Politics," *Public Policy* 24 (1976): 175-176.

7. Michael D. Reagan, *The New Federalism* (New York: Oxford Univ. Press, 1972), p. 98.

8. For a very useful categorization of the positions taken by revenue sharing's supporters see Deil S. Wright, *Understanding Intergovernmental Relations* (North Scituate, Mass.: Duxbury Press, 1978), pp. 153-154.

9. Nathan et al., *Monitoring Revenue Sharing*, pp. 347-348.

10. Excellent discussions of General Revenue Sharing's development may be found in Paul R. Dommel, *The Politics of Revenue Sharing* (Bloomington: Indiana Univ. Press, 1974); Beer, "The Adoption of General Revenue Sharing"; and Nathan et al., *Monitoring Revenue Sharing*, especially Appendix C.

11. Richard M. Nixon, "The President's Address to the Nation on Domestic Programs," *Weekly Compilation of Presidential Documents* 5 (8 August 1969): 1109-1110.

12. Nathan et al., *Monitoring Revenue Sharing*, p. 357.

13. Ibid., pp. 359-360.

14. As quoted in Caputo and Cole, *Urban Politics and Decentralization*, p. 44.

15. U.S. Department of the Treasury, Office of Revenue Sharing, *Annual Report of the Office of Revenue Sharing* (Washington, D.C.: Government Printing Office, 1974), p. 1.

16. See Nathan et al., *Monitoring Revenue Sharing*, pp. 54-62, for a lucid discussion of how the formula works.

17. As quoted in Nathan et al., *Monitoring Revenue Sharing*, p. 20.

18. Will S. Meyers, "A Legislative History of Revenue Sharing," *Annals* 419 (May 1975):11.

19. For an excellent discussion of the conditions attached to General Revenue Sharing see National Science Foundation, *General Revenue Sharing: Research Utilization Project, Volume 4, Synthesis of Impact and Process Research* (Washington, D.C.: Government Printing Office, 1975), p. 69-87 (hereafter NSF, *Synthesis of GRS Research*).

20. As quoted in Joel Havemann, "Most Powerful Lobby Faces First Test—Revenue Sharing," *National Journal Reports* 7 (1975):1718.

21. See, for example, Joel Havemann, "Revenue Sharing Plan Likely to Be Extended, Changed," *National Journal Reports* 6 (1974): 1074-1082.

22. As quoted in Joel Havemann, "It Will Be 'No-Holds-Barred' When House Takes Up Revenue Sharing," *National Journal Reports* 8 (1976): 786.

23. R.S. Reischauer, as quoted in Deil S. Wright et al., *Assessing the Impact of General Revenue Sharing in the Fifty States: A Survey of State Administrators* (Chapel Hill, N.C.: Institute for Research in the Social Sciences, University of North Carolina, 1975), pp. I-1-2 (hereafter Wright, *GRS Fifty State Survey*).

24. U.S., Department of the Treasury, Office of Revenue Sharing, *General Revenue Sharing: Reported Uses 1973-1974* (Washington, D.C.: Government Printing Office, 1975), p. 8.

25. Wright, *Understanding Intergovernmental Relations*, p. 119.

26. NSF, *Synthesis of GRS Research*, p. 66.

27. U.S., Advisory Commission on Intergovernmental Relations, *General Revenue Sharing: An ACIR Re-evaluation* (Washington, D.C.: Government Printing Office, 1974), p. 32.

28. As quoted in Patricia W. Blair, *General Revenue Sharing in American Cities: First Impressions* (Washington, D.C.: National Clearinghouse on Revenue Sharing, 1974), pp. 3-4.

29. Citations in this paragraph refer to sections of the "State and Local Fiscal Assistance Act of 1972," Public Law 92-512.

30. For an excellent summary of the literature see Donald B. Rosenthal, "Revenue Sharing and Local Governments: A Premature View of the Literature," in U.S., Congress, Senate, Committee on Government Opera-

tions, *Revenue Sharing: A Selection of Recent Research*, 94th Cong., 1st sess., March 1975, pp. 235-325 (hereafter Rosenthal, "Revenue Sharing").

31. James Fossett, "GRS and Decisionmaking in Local Government" in F. Thomas Juster, ed., *The Economic and Political Impact of General Revenue Sharing* (Washington, D.C.: Government Printing Office, 1976), p. 149.

32. Richard P. Nathan, Charles F. Adams, Jr., and associates, *Revenue Sharing: The Second Round* (Washington, D.C.: The Brookings Institution, 1977), p. 131 (hereafter Nathan et al., *GRS-Second Round*).

33. Edie Goldenberg, "Citizen Participation in General Revenue Sharing," in F. Thomas Juster, ed., *The Economic and Political Impact of General Revenue Sharing* (Washington, D.C.: Government Printing Office, 1976), p. 170.

34. NSF, *Synthesis of GRS Research*, pp. 15-16.

35. See, for example, Goldenberg, "Citizen Participation in General Revenue Sharing," p. 167; and Nathan et al., *GRS—Second Round*, p. 113.

36. Rosenthal, "Revenue Sharing," p. 269.

37. Nathan et al., *GRS—Second Round*, pp. 118-119.

38. Blair, *General Revenue Sharing in American Cities*, p. 5.

39. NSF, *Synthesis of GRS Research*, p. 60: and Juster, ed., *The Economic and Political Impact of General Revenue Sharing*, pp. 172-173.

40. See, for example, Nathan et al., *Monitoring Revenue Sharing*, p. 20.

41. For an example of the New Federalism rhetoric see U.S. Department of the Treasury, Office of Revenue Sharing, *Annual Report of the Office of Revenue Sharing*, Preface.

42. Nathan et al., *Monitoring Revenue Sharing*, pp. 24-25.

43. Havemann, "Revenue Sharing Plan Likely to Be Extended, Changed," p. 1079.

44. Morton H. Sklar, "Civil Rights under General Revenue Sharing," in National Science Foundation, *General Revenue Sharing: Research Utilization Project, Volume 2, Summaries of Impact and Process Research* (Washington, D.C.: Government Printing Office, 1975), pp. 5-22 (hereafter NSF, *Summaries of Revenue Sharing Research*).

45. Ibid., pp. 9-17.

46. As quoted in NSF, *Synthesis of GRS Research*, p. 82.

47. Havemann, "Revenue Sharing Plan Likely to Be Extended, Changed," p. 1079.

48. Nathan et al., *Monitoring Revenue Sharing*, p. 26.

49. U.S., Department of the Treasury, Office of Revenue Sharing, *Fifth Annual Report of the Office of Revenue Sharing* (Washington, D.C.: Government Printing Office, 1978), p. 3.

50. U.S., Advisory Commission on Intergovernmental Relations, *General Revenue Sharing*, p. 31.

51. NSF, *Synthesis of GRS Research*, p. 76.

52. Nathan et al., *Monitoring Revenue Sharing*, pp. 266-267.

53. NSF, *Synthesis of GRS Research*, p. 47.

54. See, for example, Thomas J. Anton et al., "Understanding the Fiscal Impact of General Revenue Sharing," in NSF, *Summaries of Revenue Sharing Research*, p. 32.

55. Nathan et al., *Monitoring Revenue Sharing*, p. 278.

56. See, for example, Havemann, "Revenue Sharing Plan Likely to Be Extended, Changed," p. 1079.

57. See, for example, Nathan et al., *Monitoring Revenue Sharing*, p. 277; and Nathan et al., *GRS—Second Round*, p. 127.

58. Blair, *General Revenue Sharing in American Cities*, p. 6.

59. Nathan et al., *GRS—Second Round*, pp. 117-118.

60. Ibid., p. 114-115; and Rosenthal, *"Revenue Sharing,"* p. 272.

61. Nathan et al., *Monitoring Revenue Sharing*, p. 278; and Nathan et al., *GRS—Second Round*, p. 267.

62. Goldenberg, "Citizen Participation in General Revenue Sharing," p. 169.

63. Steven A. Waldhorn et al., "General Revenue Sharing: Planning and Participating in Ten Large Cities," in NSF, *Summaries of Revenue Sharing Research*, p. 73.

64. Goldenberg, "Citizen Participation in General Revenue Sharing," p. 167.

65. Richard M. Nixon, "Statement on Signing the State and Local Fiscal Assistance Act of 1972," *Weekly Compilation of Presidential Documents* 8 (23 October 1972): 1535.

66. U.S. Advisory Commission on Intergovernmental Relations, *General Revenue Sharing*, p. 48.

67. Nathan et al., *GRS—Second Round*, p. 70.

68. Wright, *Understanding Intergovernmental Relations*, p. 90.

69. Ibid. for one of many comments on this problem.

70. As quoted in U.S., Congress, General Accounting Office, *Revenue Sharing: An Opportunity for Improved Public Awareness of State and Local Government Operations* (Washington, D.C.: Government Printing Office, 1975), p. 20.

71. See, for example, U.S., Congress, General Accounting Office, *Case Studies of Revenue Sharing in 26 Local Governments* (Washington, D.C.: Government Printing Office, 1975) (hereafter, GAO, *Case Studies*).

72. See, for example, Rosenthal, "Revenue Sharing," p. 247; and Nathan et al., *Monitoring Revenue Sharing*, p. 234.

73. GAO, *Case Studies*, p. 9.

74. "Should We Abandon Revenue Sharing?" *Annals* 419 (May 1975): 93.

75. See, for example, Nathan et al., *GRS—Second Round*; and Catherine Lovell and John Korey, "The Effects of GRS on Ninety-Seven Cities in Southern California" (Riverside: Univ. of California, mimeo, 1975).

76. See, for example, Wright, *GRS Fifty State Survey*; and Juster, ed., *The Economic and Political Impact of General Revenue Sharing*.

77. See, for example, Anton et al., "Understanding the Fiscal Impact of General Revenue Sharing" (Ann Arbor: Institute of Public Policy Studies, Univ. of Michigan, mimeo, 1975).

78. Ibid. Although Anton et al. conducted their analysis on data from only five jurisdictions, their results closely resemble the findings of Juster, ed., *The Economic and Political Impact of General Revenue Sharing*.

79. For a detailed discussion of the methodology see Juster, ed., *The Economic and Political Impact of General Revenue Sharing*, Appendix to Chapter 2.

80. F. Thomas Juster, "Fiscal Impacts on Local Governments," in Ibid., p. 38.

81. These data are reported in Allen Manvel, "The Fiscal Impact of Revenue Sharing," *Annals* 419 (May 1975): 41.

82. Nathan et al., *Monitoring Revenue Sharing*, p. 199.

83. Nathan et al., *GRS—Second Round*, pp. 35, 52.

84. See Juster, ed., *The Economic and Political Impact of General Revenue Sharing*, Appendix to Chapter 3, for details on the methodology.

85. Wright, *Understanding Intergovernmental Relations*, p. 118.

86. NSF, *Synthesis of GRS Research*, p. 41.

87. See, for example, Morton H. Sklar, "The Impact of Revenue Sharing on Minorities and the Poor," *Harvard Civil Rights-Civil Liberties Review* 10 (January 1975):93-136.

88. See Juster, ed., *The Economic and Political Impact of General Revenue Sharing*, pp. 65-66.

89. Blair, *General Revenue Sharing in American Cities*, p. 20.

90. Nathan et al., *GRS—Second Round*, p. 91.

91. Ibid., p. 75.

92. Fossett, "GRS and Decisionmaking in Local Government," p. 153.

93. NSF, *Synthesis of GRS Research*, p. 96.

94. Fossett, "GRS and Decisionmaking in Local Government," p. 155.

95. Nathan et al., *GRS—Second Round*, p. 57.

96. Nathan et al., *Monitoring Revenue Sharing*, p. 154.

97. Wright,, *Understanding Intergovernmental Relations*, p. 91.

98. As reported in Fossett, "GRS and Decision-making in Local Government," p. 155.

99. Nathan et al., *Monitoring Revenue Sharing*, pp. 267-277.

100. Blair, *General Revenue Sharing in American Cities*, p. 21.

101. Rosenthal, "Revenue Sharing," pp. 282-283.

102. Caputo and Cole, *Urban Politics and Decentralization*, p. 70.

103. Sarah F. Liebschutz, "General Revenue Sharing as a Political Resource for Local Officials," in Charles O. Jones and Robert D. Thomas, eds., *Public Policy Making in a Federal System* (Beverly Hills: Sage Publications, 1976), p. 112.

104. See, for example, Caputo and Cole, *Urban Politics and Decentralization,* p. 114; Nathan et al., *Monitoring Revenue Sharing*, pp. 220-222; Nathan et al., *GRS—Second Round*, p. 34.

105. Rosenthal, "Revenue Sharing," p. 256.

106. Nathan et al., *GRS—Second Round*, p. 74.

107. Caputo and Cole, *Urban Politics and Decentralization*, pp. 102-103.

108. Goldenberg, "Citizen Participation in General Revenue Sharing," p. 181.

109. Nathan et al., *GRS—Second Round*, p. 50.

110. Goldenberg, "Citizen Participation in General Revenue Sharing," p. 182.

3

CETA: Jobs, Training, and Politics

The Comprehensive Employment and Training Act (CETA), enacted in late 1973 after several years of debate over manpower reform in Congress, has changed dramatically since its original authorization. In fiscal year 1975, its first year of operation, state and local government spent $3.8 billion on CETA programs; by fiscal year 1978 that figure had grown 112 percent to $8.1 billion. In addition to the rapid increase in funding, CETA experienced a shift in emphasis. From a program whose avowed purpose was to train the chronically unemployed, it primarily became a program to alleviate high unemployment rates during a deep economic recession. Alarmed by the steady growth in the unemployment rate from around 4 percent at its initial passage to consistent rates over 7 percent, Congress enlarged CETA's public service employment component from 100,000 jobs in its first year to 725,000 jobs in fiscal year 1978.[1]

Although CETA started out with bipartisan support in 1973, when President Nixon called it "one of the finest pieces of legislation to come to my desk this year,"[2] five years later, during its major reauthorization fight, it was attacked by former supporters as well as longtime critics as "the second most unpopular program in the country, after welfare."[3] As essential background to understanding and analyzing CETA, it is important to examine the details of its enactment and the history of its transformation.

A Legislative History of CETA

Before the 1960s, the federal government's most prominent role in employment and training policy came during the Depression of the 1930s when the Works Progress Administration, created in 1935, employed over 3 million people at its peak and averaged $1.4 billion in expenditures from 1935 to 1943.[4] During the War on Poverty of the 1960s the term "manpower policy" again entered the public policy lexicon. At that time the federal government's programs were "designed to improve the employability and enhance employment and earnings prospects of persons . . . suffering various disadvantages in competition for jobs."[5]

CETA's legislative history covers a twenty-year period that can be divided into four somewhat overlapping periods. During the first phase, federal manpower programs developed one by one as Congress recognized the value of programs that would serve varying needs and constituencies. Within a few years, by the mid-1960s, some members of Congress and federal executives began calling for reform and consolidation of the overlapping programs. These efforts culminated in CETA's enactment and constitute the second period of its history. The third major phase in CETA's development was characterized by substantial growth in its public service employment programs and a general return to the narrow-gauge programs of the 1960s. The final period includes Congress's reauthorization and reorientation of the CETA program in 1978.

Between 1961 and 1973 seventeen so-called categorical manpower programs were enacted by Congress. They shared the common goal of enhancing the employment prospects of the chronically unemployed, but each focused on a specific clientele, such as youth, older workers, or veterans, and each was implemented through a unique set of local educational and community organizations.[6] The most important programs of the categorical era are described here.

The Area Redevelopment Act of 1961 provided assistance to industries willing to relocate in economically depressed areas and distributed aid to unemployed people living there.

The Manpower Development and Training Act of 1962 established retraining programs for middle-aged workers displaced by technological change. The $100 million program was administered by the Department of Labor through local vocational schools. With unemployment among youth and minorities up to 15 percent in 1963, Congress shifted MDTA's emphasis to younger trainees.

The Economic Opportunity Act of 1964 authorized education, training, and work experience programs for impoverished youth and included the Job Corps, a program of intensive vocational skills training, and the Neighborhood Youth Corps, which provided part-time jobs for high-school students and dropouts. As part of the Johnson administration's War on Poverty, Community Action Agencies were established apart from existing structures of local government to run the programs. Work experience programs for the rural poor were subsequently added through "Operation Mainstream." The New Careers program for education and employability development was also added later.

The Emergency Employment Act of 1971 provided $2.25 billion for 200,000 public sector jobs over a two-year period. It was the first federal manpower program to put local elected officials in charge of resource allocation and thus foreshadowed the CETA program, which accomplished this goal for a wider range of employment and training programs.[7]

During the late 1960s and early 1970s Congress, executive branch officials, and various interest groups attempted to improve the effectiveness of the employment and training programs that had multiplied haphazardly.[8]

Their efforts resulted in the passage of CETA, but not without a number of trials and errors. One of the earliest reform efforts occurred in 1967 when Congress directed Community Action Agencies to coordinate all employment and training programs. The intent was to make such programs comprehensive by placing them under the control of a single sponsor. In this way Congress hoped to remedy the overlapping layers of programs at the local level that increased administrative overhead and bewildered potential applicants. Though these early efforts were only mildly successful, experience gained through them helped shape the design of CETA.

One of the U.S. Department of Labor's important administrative reforms established Cooperative Area Manpower Planning Systems (CAMPS) to address the problem of coordination. CAMPS committees united federal, state, and local government agencies with private nonprofit program operators, the business sector, and organized labor in order to plan employment and training programs for their communities. Nine federal agencies, who at the time were administering the various categorical manpower programs, agreed to cooperate in the CAMPS venture, but none relinquished control over their programs. State Employment Services directed the CAMPS planning committees that numbered 400 by 1971. Unfortunately, CAMPS fell short of the Department of Labor's expectations. According to Secretary of Labor George Schultz, the utility of the plans produced by the CAMPS committees was "limited to the use of a common staple to hold individual requests together."[9] They failed to simplify the Byzantine structure of categorical programs because the committees had limited staff, no real control over the allocation of federal program funds, and no leverage to make individual program operators cooperate with one another.

Comprehensive legislative proposals for reshaping employment and training programs were made in 1969 and 1970. But none of the bills gained congressional approval because of differences between the Congress, the administration of President Nixon, and interest groups over how to divide responsibility for running the programs, and whether there should be a federally funded public jobs program. Everyone agreed that some breakup of the restrictive categorical programs was necessary; however, how far the legislation should go to accomplish that goal produced controversy.[10]

The public service jobs issue separated congressional Democrats, who favored the idea, from the Republican administration, which was strongly opposed to it. In 1970, in large part because it authorized a public service employment program, President Nixon vetoed one Democratically backed manpower reform bill and his veto was sustained in the Senate.[11] But the following year he signed an Emergency Employment Act (described above) funding public service jobs in local governments. According to one observer, President Nixon agreed to sign the bill only after he had extracted "promises that both houses would move rapidly to consider comprehensive manpower legislation."[12]

President Nixon called for manpower revenue sharing in 1971, as part of the broader New Federalism initiatives. He characterized the administration of employment and training programs as "overcentralized, bureaucratic, remote from the people they mean to serve, overguidelined, and far less effective than they might be in helping the unskilled and the disadvantaged." Saying that the programs did "not belong in federal hands," Nixon proposed a formula grant for broad purpose manpower programs operated by state and local governments with reduced "interference" by the Department of Labor.[13] Congressional Democrats refused to eliminate federal oversight, however, and insisted that public service jobs be included to cope with a swelling jobless population.

The confrontation between the administration and the Congress peaked in 1973. Frustrated over congressional inaction, the administration abandoned its efforts to achieve legislative manpower reform. The Office of Management and Budget reported: "Administrative requirements under existing law will be modified to allow the States and localities to group manpower services in ways that best meet local needs, and to choose the organizations to operate these programs. Manpower revenue sharing will be achieved administratively. . .and will build on the [CAMPS]."[14] Draft regulations for implementing the administration's plan were prepared to transfer various categorical programs from community organizations such as the Urban League and Community Action Agencies to mayors and county officials. Public service employment programs authorized by the Emergency Employment Act were also scheduled for termination.

Congressional and interest group reaction to the administration's plan was swift and sharply critical. Lobbies for state and local governments, such as the National Association of Counties and the National League of Cities, strongly preferred legislation that would protect them from capricious actions by the Department of Labor. Agencies operating the categorical programs, such as the Urban League and the Opportunities Industrialization Centers, marshaled protestors to demonstrate on Capitol Hill against the proposal. The House Subcommittee on Manpower reported out legislation blocking the administration's manpower revenue sharing. The Senate quickly passed an extension of the Emergency Employment Act.

Finally, in late 1973, a bargain was struck among the administration, leading manpower experts in the House and Senate, and major interest groups. The Senators and House members agreed to postpone the Emergency Employment Act extension, which the administration vehemently opposed. The administration halted efforts to bring about manpower reform without legislation. It also acceded to the request by Democrats for a public service jobs program funded at $250 million in fiscal year 1974 and agreed to preserve a significant federal role in approving local manpower plans and monitoring performance. In return the administration obtained a bill that would eliminate most of the categorical programs authorized in the preceding dozen years and would place state and local elected officials in control of employment and training programs in their political jurisdictions.

William Bechtal, executive director of the Wisconsin State Manpower Planning Council, concisely summarized the series of concessions that produced an acceptable compromise on CETA:

> When this manpower debate began—with the introduction of the Administration's Manpower Training Act in 1969—Governors, Vocational Educators, and the State Employment Service all were arguing for a near dominant role in manpower programs. All three have made tremendous concessions in the interest of resolving a stalemate on this issue. Almost every city and county would really like to be directly funded. . .but most of them have come to accept the. . .cutoff somewhere around 100,000 or 150,000 population. Community Action Agencies and private, nonprofit groups have largely dropped their insistence that specific funds be earmarked for them. The Secretary of Labor and his regional manpower offices, have. . .made tremendous concessions, offering to yield much of their authority. . . . The Administration has yielded significantly on retaining aspects of the Emergency Employment Act.[15]

In late December 1973 President Nixon signed the Comprehensive Employment and Training Act. Title I of the act established comprehensive employment and training services to be administered by "prime sponsors," for the most part states and units of local government with 100,000 or more residents. Title II authorized a public service employment program for areas with 6.5 percent or higher unemployment rates for three consecutive months. Title III placed various programs for youth, Native Americans, migrant workers, and others under the control of the Department of Labor. Title IV preserved the Job Corps program created in the mid-1960s and also put it under federal administration. Other titles authorized a National Commission for Manpower Policy and outlined general administrative provisions, including prohibitions against discrimination and political activities by program administrators or their clients.[16] Table 3-1 shows CETA's budget from fiscal year 1975 to fiscal year 1978.

Within six months of CETA's commencement, the national unemployment rate rose from approximately 4 percent when CETA passed to 7 percent, its highest point in thirteen years. Congress quickly approved an expanded public service employment program, known as the Emergency Jobs and Unemployment Assistance Act of 1974. President Ford signed the bill, authorizing $2.5 billion over an eighteen-month period. Grafted on as Title VI of CETA, the new law was the first stage in the massive expansion of public service employment under CETA. Combined spending for public service employment programs in CETA's first year just about equaled the funds earmarked for the Title I comprehensive service programs.[17] Three

Table 3-1
Summary of CETA Appropriations for Fiscal Years 1975-1978
(in millions of dollars)

CETA Programs	1975	1976	1977	1978
Title I: Comprehensive Manpower Services	1,580	1,580	1,880	1,880
Title II: Public Employment Programs	400	1,520	524	1,016
Title III: National Programs	239	233	609	388
Summer Youth	548	528	595	693
Title III-C and VIII: Special Youth Program	–	–	1,000	–
Title IV: Job Corps	175	175	265	417
Title VI: Emergency Job Program	875	1,625	3,179	3,668
Totals	3,817	5,661	8,052	8,052

Sources: U.S., Library of Congress, Congressional Research Service, "The Comprehensive Employment and Training Act, As Amended by the Comprehensive Employment and Training Act Amendments of 1978," Report No. 78-252 EPW (prepared by Robert M. Guttman), December 19, 1978, p. CRS-8. Additional data from the Employment and Training Administration, U.S. Department of Labor.

years later, in fiscal year 1978, public service employment programs were 2.5 times larger than Title I.

Title VI had a different purpose than did Title II, which also authorized public service jobs. Title II provided temporary employment for people who had been out of work for thirty days or more. In the language of manpower experts, Title II was aimed at the long-term or structurally unemployed, people who lack the training and experience to get and keep jobs even when the economy is booming. In contrast, Title VI was supposed to serve the short-term or countercyclically unemployed, people who were laid off due to the downturn in the national economy. Consequently one could be enrolled in a Title VI public service job after two weeks of unemployment in a community with a 7 percent unemployment rate.[18]

Nearly two years later, after sustained periods of high unemployment, Congress again expanded and altered the public service employment components of CETA. By appropriating $6.6 billion in May of 1977, Congress supplied enough funds to boost enrollments in Titles II and VI from 310,000 recipients in October 1976 to 725,000 in March 1978. Fearing that the federally funded public service jobs might displace jobs in the private sector and that state and local governments were substituting CETA funds for their own revenues, Congress took steps to avoid such negative effects. The revised statute required prime sponsors to develop "PSE projects" with the additional money beyond the amount needed to sustain current public service employees. The PSE projects had to be activities that could not be completed without federal jobs money.

The new law also restricted participation in the PSE projects to the economically disadvantaged and long-term unemployed.[19] Because of the new entrance standards, according to one analyst at the Brookings Institution, "The initially countercyclical Title VI programs now [had] the eligibility requirements of a more structurally oriented program, and the initially structurally oriented Title II program now [had] the minimal eligibility requirements more characteristic of the countercyclical program."[20]

In 1976 Congress also initiated a gradual trend of recategorizing employment and training programs. In other words, it authorized specific programs for particular clienteles, supplementing the broad block grant. For example, in 1976 two such programs, the Skills Training and Improvement Program (STIP) for experienced workers who were unemployed and in need of advanced training, and the Help through Industry Retraining and Employment (HIRE) program to assist veterans through on-the-job training, were added onto Title III of CETA.

Responding to high unemployment rates among young people, Congress continued this trend by creating two more categorical youth programs in 1977. The Youth Employment and Demonstration Projects Act, folded into Title III of CETA, authorized $1 billion for a host of experimental youth employment and training projects, most of which would be handled by state and local prime sponsors. A new Title VIII of CETA establishing a Young Adult Conservation Corps, modeled after the Civilian Conservation Corps of the 1930s, offered work on conservation and wildlife projects for over 20,000 young people.[21]

Table 3-1 displays the budgetary growth of all CETA programs between fiscal year 1975 and fiscal year 1978. Significantly, the major increases occurred in the special purpose programs, where congressional and federal control is highest, rather than in the Title I program, where local government prime sponsors have the most discretion.

Though the original statute was, by 1977, staggering under all its amendments, Congress postponed a comprehensive reauthorization by passing a one-year extension of the law that year. Therefore the first major overhaul of CETA did not occur until late in 1978. Important alterations were made. Public service employment jobs were reduced from the previously authorized level of 725,000 to 660,000; narrow eligibility requirements for participation in CETA programs were extended to nearly all the law's programs; greater emphasis on developmental programs such as classroom training was encouraged; and more involvement by representatives of the private sector was required.[22] Table 3-2 presents fiscal year 1979 appropriations for the revised law.

Table 3-2

Summary of CETA Appropriations for Fiscal Year 1979[a]

(in millions of dollars)

CETA Programs under 1978 Reauthorization	Amount
Title II:	
Parts A, B, and C: Comprehensive Employment and Training Services	1,914
Part D: Transitional Public Service Employment for the Economically Disadvantaged	2,517
Title III: Special Federal Programs	372
Title IV:	
Part A: Youth Employment Demonstration Program	714
Part B: Job Corps	296
Part C: Summber Youth Programs	740
Title VI: Countercyclical Public Service Employment	3,475
Title VII: Private Sector Initiative Program	—
Title VIII: Young Adult Conservation Corps	217
Total	10,245

Source: U.S., Library of Congress, Congressional Research Service, "The Comprehensive Employment and Training Act, As Amended by the Comprehensive Employment and Training Act Amendments of 1978," Report No. 78-252 EPW (prepared by Robert M. Guttman) December 19, 1978, p. CRS-9.

[a]These figures are from a continuing appropriation for fiscal year 1979. Title VII, the Private Sector Program, could not receive funds under the continuing appropriation because it was a new program and thus did not have a funding level to continue but President Carter made a supplemental appropriation request of $400 million for this program for fiscal year 1979.

Summary

In less than five years, CETA was substantially transformed: its budget more than doubled; four important amendments added new programs and restructured existing ones; public service employment, originally a minor part of CETA, eventually dwarfed other program components; and broad eligibility requirements were gradually narrowed and then abandoned in favor of relatively restrictive ones stressing enrollment of the poor and long-term unemployed. Yet the basic structure of CETA was intact. It was still run by state and local governments with limited and only slightly increased federal oversight. Its original mission seemed to have been restored: once again CETA was placing emphasis on the structurally unemployed.

Implementing CETA: What Happened and Why?

CETA is a multipurpose law with a variety of specific programs and complex requirements. In order to place reasonable boundaries on the analysis,

I have chosen to evaluate four fundamental questions about CETA's performance: who governs, what is the impact of decategorization, how are PSE jobs distributed, and who benefits from the jobs and training? The largest and most significant CETA programs, those authorized by Titles I, II, and VI, will be the focus of my assessment. Finally, I will pay primary attention to the implementation of the original legislation and programs added during the period of rapid expansion from 1974 to 1978. The impact of the 1978 reauthorization was not felt until after its provisions were implemented in the spring of 1979. Each section in the remainder of the chapter considers how the policy's goals were handled during legislative deliberations; the extent to which they were subsequently modified; the empirical evidence on program performance; and the factors that account for it.

Who Governs? The Role of Local Elected
Officials, Citizens, and the Federal Government

Nearly all participants in CETA's legislative history agreed that the structure of programs developed during the categorical era was inflexible and minimally productive. Reform legislation introduced from 1969 to 1973 by Democrats and Republicans alike proposed program consolidation. On two other issues, however, there were serious disagreements: the number and character of public service jobs, and the goal of decentralization—making local elected officials responsible for administering the program.

Recalling the development of CETA, Daniel Krivit, chief counsel to the House Subcommittee on Labor, observed that there was general consensus on the goal of breaking up the categorical system, but "the real problem was . . . how the power was to be distributed between the various levels of government."[23] Labor Secretary Hodgeson stated the administration's argument for decentralizing power to local officials during hearings on the administration's manpower bill in 1972:

> The rigid, categorical approach of our present system provides few options to State and local officials . . . and inhibits responsive action with redtape and paperwork related to Federal standards and guidelines. . . . Manpower services should be in response to the needs of the individual. Those needs are best perceived and responded to where the individual lives. So local responsiveness must be combined with federal resources. . . .[24]

Democratic majorities in the House and Senate preferred limited decentralization and vigorous oversight. Responding to Secretary Hodgeson, Representative Dominick Daniels, chairman of the Subcommittee on Labor, expressed concern over programs run by local authorities: "I don't think [that the money] should be shovelled out to a Governor or to a mayor . . . for him to spend in any manner, shape, or form that he desires. . . . I feel that the legislation does not go far enough insofar as accountability is concerned."[25]

Eventually the administration and Democratic leaders on Capitol Hill compromised on decentralization, but, far from removing federal oversight, CETA mandated an important role for the federal government. The Department of Labor, through its ten regional offices, was given responsibility for reviewing plans of state and local government prime sponsors, collecting information, evaluating the performance of prime sponsors, and providing technical assistance. The statute delegated broad authority to state and local officials, prescribed substantial federal responsibilities, and left room for a great deal of interpretation.

The debate over citizen participation in CETA programs was less intense, since Congress and the administration paid scant attention to the issue; yet the potential role of manpower planning councils was significant. As authorized by CETA, each prime sponsor must appoint an advisory council composed of citizens representing community organizations, organized labor, and the business sector. The planning council's job is to advise the elected officials ". . . regarding program plans and basic goals, policies, and procedures, [and] to monitor and provide for objective evaluations" (Section 104).[26] Though the law suggested categories of people that should be appointed and the general scope of the council's activities, it limited the council's role to advice: the chief elected official in the prime sponsorship was ultimately responsible for CETA's implementation.

Elected Officials

Substantial evidence from studies of prime sponsors indicates that mayors, governors, and county executives, though more heavily involved in making manpower decisions under CETA than under its precursor, CAMPS, were not influential in all types of CETA programs.[27] With limited time available, they intervened primarily in decisions involving dollar allocations. A study conducted by Ohio State University researchers in seventeen prime sponsors found that elected officials participated most often in the selection of contractors to run employment and training programs and in decisions about how much money should be devoted to Title I Public Service Employment Programs. In most other decisions about the block grant Title I programs, the professional staff was dominant.[28]

Both the Ohio State study and a study by the National Academy of Sciences (NAS), which was conducted in twenty-four prime sponsorships, concluded that political officials usually controlled the allocation of public service employment funds.[29] These decisions were most important for the political jurisdictions because they determined whether federally funded public service employees would perform jobs for city or county agencies or whether private, nonprofit agencies would be supported.

Manpower Planning Councils

The principal vehicle for citizen participation in CETA programs was the Manpower Planning Councils. According to the Ohio State University and NAS studies, the councils ranged from being unimportant in some local governments to being extremely important in a few. In some areas, advisory councils were appointed by the elected officials, met once, and then were virtually disbanded. In contrast, some planning councils practically seized control of the local employment and training programs.

Overall, the Ohio State analysts judged that the manpower planning councils were involved most often in discussions of general employment and training goals and least often in concrete decisions, such as which agencies should receive contracts or how much money should be devoted to vocational training programs versus youth work experience projects. Moreover, the councils tended to have little or no influence over the shape of public service employment programs in their communities.[30] According to the National Academy of Sciences study, however, planning councils were important across a full range of issues in at least a few prime sponsorships. Indeed, they concluded that planning councils had a "substantial effect" in one-third of the cities and counties included in their study.[31]

Manpower planning councils, which were supposed to serve as representatives of the community, were primarily made up of people with a vested interest in CETA funds. Forty percent of all planning council members in the Ohio prime sponsorships were either representatives of agencies providing employment and training services or city and county government officials. Very few individuals enrolled in employment and training programs had been appointed to the councils.[32] Because the memberships were loaded down with agency representatives fighting for a share of the available CETA dollars, manpower planning council deliberations often degenerated into self-serving logrolling sessions, where agencies would agree to support each other when their contracts were up for review.[33] In such an environment, objective evaluations of employment and training programs were unlikely.

The Federal Role

The Employment and Training Administration of the U.S. Department of Labor (DOL), which had managed the pre-CETA categorical programs through individual contracts with educational and community organizations, was responsible for overseeing the decentralized CETA program. A study by the author indicates that during the first two years of CETA's implementation the DOL had difficulty carrying out its responsibilities and often acted counterproductively.[34] It paid only limited attention to CETA's major goals such as what groups were receiving employment and training services, concentrating instead on less controversial matters. It monitored the production of reports on program expenditures and participant enrollment, for instance, but rarely analyzed their content in order to recommend corrective actions. The federal role, during CETA's early years, was also vacillating and confusing to local prime sponsors. Labor's directions to state and local government changed with dismaying frequency. Perhaps DOL's only consistent policy was its insistence that grants be expended rapidly in order to stimulate the lagging national economy.

Over time, however, because of the growth of public service employment, widespread allegations of local political scandal and corruption, pressure from members of Congress, and a turnover in national administration, the department attempted to intervene more in local decisions. Under Secretary Ray Marshall, appointed by a Democratic president and not devoted to the original motion of decentralized CETA programs, DOL moved quickly to "assert more federal control over the country's main manpower delivery system."[35] By the late 1970s, local government officials were complaining that the department had overstepped its authority and reneged on its commitment to local autonomy.

Explaining Who Governs: The Model Applied

Elected officials put more time and attention into CETA funded employment and training programs than they ever had before, but they concentrated on only a few major issues, such as the nature and scope of the public service employment programs in their jurisdiction. Citizen participation through the mandated manpower planning councils varied greatly in significance from one community to another, but the council's roles were typically limited and their deliberations dominated by program contractors and government officials rather than disinterested citizens. Initially, the federal government's role in CETA was relatively passive but changeable, contributing to confusion in program administration. Under the Carter administration, however, the Department of Labor became much more assertive in guiding state and local government CETA programs.

Policy Standards and Resources. The policy standards were not by themselves very influential in determining CETA governance patterns. Rather, they established a wide range of acceptable actions by elected officials, manpower planning councils, and the federal government. Nevertheless, several features of the statute and its resources are worth noting.

1. The increased interest in CETA programs displayed by local elected officials was a direct response to the 1,000 percent increase in public service employment funds from the initial program in early 1974 to the spring of 1978. The rapid infusion of dollars for hiring public service employees provided local officials with an irresistible opportunity to dispense jobs to large numbers of people and to expand the scope of public services in their communities. By 1978 CETA public service employees often staffed a significant portion of the local government's agencies, including such essential services as police, fire protection, and sanitation.

2. The statute provided a broad but vague mandate for manpower planning councils. Their tasks were considerable; their authority was limited. Consequently, despite the rhetoric of citizen participation surrounding the law, the policy's standards did little to foster it or to guide elected officials and their staffs in the use of manpower planning councils.

3. The statute authorized federal intervention in the local affairs of prime sponsors, but also put local officials in charge of running CETA programs. Given such vague and contradictory guidelines, it is not surprising that the federal role could vacillate during the course of CETA's implementation, even with no amendments to the basic statutory provisions for federal oversight.

The National Policy Environment. The national policy environment[36] does more than the policy standards and resources to explain the roles of elected officials and citizens, and is most important in accounting for the federal government's changing influence on CETA.

1. The national and regional staff of the Department of Labor paid scant attention to the involvement of local elected officials or manpower planning councils in CETA decision-making. According to one senior DOL official, involving political officials and worrying about citizen participation were "just not our highest priorities in CETA. We were too busy with public service employment and other problems, such as how to spend all the money."[37] So busy were they, in fact, that they frequently approved the plans of state and local governments who ignored citizen participation almost entirely.

2. In large part, the department's wavering leadership was caused, on both the national and regional levels, by pressure from external groups such as the Congress trying to influence CETA's implementation. Ambiguities about the federal government's responsibilities and power persisted after the law was passed, and, as a result, efforts to affect DOL's role in implementation persisted as well.

Congress, or more precisely the dozen or so congressmen and congressional staffers most knowledgeable and concerned about employment and training programs, gave conflicting orders to the Department of Labor on how to handle the CETA program. Republicans criticized the department for overmanaging CETA and were supported by various interest groups representing state and local officials, such as the U.S. Conference of Mayors and the National Association of Counties. Congressional Democrats, advancing the position they had taken during CETA's legislative history, pressured DOL to actively manage CETA. Their position was reinforced by demands for strong federal intervention by pre-CETA categorical contractors such as the Opportunities Industrialization Centers and the Urban League, and by local government employee unions.

Operating in this volatile environment, the national office of the Department of Labor behaved in a confusing and contradictory manner from the perspective of a local prime sponsor. On some issues, such as the implementation of public service jobs programs, the department aggressively carried out its policy of rapid expansion. On other issues, such as who should benefit from CETA or how local delivery systems should be structured, the DOL made almost no attempt to intervene in local decisions. Contradiction and delay prevented a clear understanding of federal intent.

The new presidential administration and the general reorientation of CETA programs explain the increased federal intervention in 1977 and 1978. The narrow categorical programs added to CETA in these years are usually operated by state and local governments, but they carried with them more specific national goals and more intrusive federal requirements, giving the federal government an opportunity to exert more control over local choices. Moreover, the Carter administration favored stronger federal oversight and control. Although the federal government has tried to strengthen its control over CETA programs, however, it is not certain that these efforts have always succeeded.

The Local Policy Environment. The most important factors accounting for patterns of local decision-making were features of the local policy environment.

1. Elected officials' participation in CETA programs was influenced by their orientations toward CETA, by local economic conditions, and by the fiscal condition of their city or county. Among the elected officials who devoted considerable attention to CETA, some expected to derive political benefits from the recession relief program; others feared damaging consequences if they ignored CETA and it later became caught up in scandal; still others were drawn into the program by community groups demanding CETA contracts or jobs. Not all officials were involved for these negative or self-interested reasons, however. Occasionally they seized the opportunity

presented by the CETA program to improve their community's public services and supported their staff's efforts to mount effective employment training programs.[38]

Rising unemployment rates in many cities and counties also affected not only the actions of political officials but also their orientations toward CETA. One mayor of a medium-sized city with high unemployment rates described his discovery of CETA: "When unemployment is low, a manpower division is just another agency: now it is important because of the unemployment problem. The benefits are spread around and the programs are a political asset."[39] Finally, fiscal crises in some jurisdictions aroused elected officials' interest in CETA. Some officials used CETA funds to hire local government personnel who had been laid off. During such crises, political officials usually assumed direct control of the public service employment program or delegated it to a close deputy.[40]

2. The impact of manpower planning councils was shaped by the attitudes and involvement of elected officials and by the composition of the councils. Where the staff and elected officials opposed an active planning council there was virtually no chance that the council would be influential. Where political officials were active, the councils tended to be insignificant. Frequently, staff members and elected officials complained that planning councils (which they appointed) were collections of self-interested individuals who could not be trusted to make fair decisions. Of course, staff and elected officials did occasionally encourage meaningful council participation, particularly when the council could legitimate controversial decisions. Consequently, many planning councils acted as political buffers for mayors and county executives. For example, many advisory councils were used in the spring of 1977 to help dole out large sums of money for public service employment projects. Disaffected organizations that did not receive grants thus directed their anger at the planning council rather than at the elected officials.[41]

The membership of the council was also important in determining its role. Councils made up of a large percentage of agencies operating CETA-funded programs tended to be active and sometimes influential because their members had strong incentives to participate. After appointing a contractor-dominated council, elected officials who were uninterested in CETA often delegated the problems associated with allocating CETA dollars to them.[42] There were also active councils composed of civic-minded business and labor representatives whose only interest in CETA was to help make the program work better, but these kinds of councils appeared less frequently.

3. The federal government's impact on prime sponsors was determined partially by the general orientations of local political officials and their staffs. Some officials accepted the legitimacy of federal oversight and in-

tervention and were willing to abide by it. Others rejected federal "meddling" in local decisions and either openly resisted the department's initiatives or, more typically, listened to the federal directives and then ignored them.[43]

Summary

The varying activity and influence of elected officials and citizen advisory groups are explained by characteristics of the local policy environment, including the actors' general perceptions of the importance of CETA, which were often influenced by the local economy and the fiscal condition of the governmental jurisdiction. The changing role of the federal government during CETA's implementation is explained by the ongoing debate in the national policy environment over the proper role of the Department of Labor. The policy standards and resources were the least significant factor in accounting for governance patterns, because they permitted wide latitude for local determination. But the tremendous increase in public service employment funds made political officials take notice of CETA and in many cases led to control by elected officials of the PSE aspects of the program.

What Is the Impact of Decategorization?
Program Design and Expenditures

Among the principal arguments in favor of CETA's passage was the need for reform in methods of delivering manpower programs. Proponents of reform, those supporting "decategorization" or a breakup of the narrowly drawn employment and training programs of the 1960s, argued that twelve years of haphazard lawmaking had produced duplicative programs with no administrative control. Moreover, they charged that the federal government lacked sufficient knowledge of local conditions and needs to make rational choices for the design of locally based programs. Folding all the categorical programs into a broad block grant and putting them under a single local authority, they thought, would remedy the management nightmares of the categorical era.

Opponents of decategorization agreed that local flexibility was desirable but feared that programs developed by the federal government and supported by Congress would be dismantled by state and local officials for political reasons. In the words of Senator Gaylord Nelson, chairman of the Subcommittee on Employment, Manpower, and Poverty during the development of CETA, "Some of these programs. . .were developed over the objections of city hall or State Governors and if we throw the control back there all of a sudden, what might happen to some of them?''[44] Other senators who shared this concern attempted to set aside funds in CETA for certain programs and community organizations such as the Opportunities Industrialization Centers, but the provision was deleted in the conference between the House and the Senate and thus did not become law.

CETA authorizes state and local officials to restructure employment and training programs and includes a laundry list of eligible activities for funding. Thus, despite the rhetoric at the time of CETA's enactment, the law itself was largely silent on how local government prime sponsors might accomplish reform. The analysis considers the effects of decategorization under Title I—the block grant component of CETA—including alterations in methods for delivering employment and training programs, changes in the rosters of agencies chosen to run them, and the kinds of employment and training programs that are funded.

Methods of Program Delivery

Prior to CETA, the federal government contracted directly with local educational institutions and other nonprofit organizations to carry out categorical employment and training programs. Each agency contractor recruited, trained, and placed its own clientele. This approach to program delivery often caused duplication, inadequate service for some people in need of training, and inappropriate services for others. For instance, someone walking into a program for training auto body repairmen might find himself enrolled in that program whether he needed that kind of training or not. Agencies competed with each other to fill up their training slots: referrals from one agency to another were rare. Lacking any single coordinating authority, the structure of employment and training programs in most communities before CETA was highly fragmented.

CETA gave state and local governments the authority to coordinate employment and training programs, to improve the system by restructuring or eliminating existing approaches in their communities. Accurately assessing the overall change in program delivery since the introduction of CETA is extremely difficult. But two national studies suggest that new approaches for delivering comprehensive, integrated employment and training programs were developed only minimally. Defining comprehensive program deliveries as a unification, centralization, and coordination of all manpower services in a single geographic area, the National Academy of Sciences found only four such prime sponsors in their group of twenty-four during CETA's first year. Only one-third became "comprehensive" in the second year.[45]

Examining fifteen different prime sponsors from 1976 to 1977, CETA's third year, analysts at the Ohio State University observed similar outcomes. In most of the prime sponsors in their study, participants were unable to move among different employment and training programs or among programs funded under different titles of the act; that is, programs were not "integrated." Only one prime sponsor's program was highly integrated; in six there was some integration, and eight had made no attempt to achieve reform.[46]

Measured at the broadest levels change in the methods for delivering employment and training programs was marginal. Nevertheless new approaches were tried in many prime sponsors and some achieved substantially improved programs. One of the most common changes was the adoption of central intake systems whereby a person seeking employment and training services is "guaranteed access to all program components."[47] Eleven of the twenty-four prime sponsors analyzed by the National Academy of Sciences adopted the central intake approach in order to gain more control over their programs.

Choices of Agencies to Deliver Programs

CETA programs can be operated by a range of agencies including boards of education, Community Action Agencies, proprietary schools, state employment services, and, of course, departments of the city or county government. Elected officials were given the option under CETA of continuing contracts with the agencies that had run manpower programs during the categorical era or writing new contracts with an entirely different set of agencies. On the first day of CETA's implementation, local elected officials inherited the existing structure of program operators in their communities. Prime sponsors desiring new organizations would have to eliminate or modify contracts with those agencies and incur the consequences.

The National Academy of Sciences and the Ohio State University studies of CETA provide evidence on the choices made by prime sponsors. Table 3-3, adapted from the NAS study, shows that overall, only state employment service offices, long the presumptive deliverers of manpower programs, experienced a substantial loss in the transition to CETA. Despite dire predictions to the contrary, community organizations, such as the Opportunities Industrialization Centers, maintained a stable percentage of the total CETA resources and increased their expenditures by nearly $50 million over the categorical period. "Other deliverers," namely the prime sponsor agencies, operated additional employment and training programs under the CETA system. The Ohio State study found similar results when it compared the agencies running programs in CETA's first and second years.

Table 3-3

CETA, Title I Expenditures by Various Types of Delivery Agencies for Fiscal Years 1974 and 1976[a]

(in millions of dollars and percent)

Type of Agency	1974		1976	
	Amount	*Percent*	*Amount*	*Percent*
Community organizations (OIC, Urban League, SER)	46	12	95	13
State employment service	90	23	67	10
Education agencies	162	41	271	39
Other deliverers[b]	93	24	265	38
Totals	391	100	698	100

Source: Based on data from the Employment and Training Administration, U.S. Department of Labor. Reproduced from *CETA: Manpower Programs under Local Control* (1978), page 146, with the permission of the National Academy of Sciences, Washington, D.C.

[a]Includes 5 percent vocational educational grants to states and excludes expenditures for wages, allowances, and fringe benefits to program participants.

[b]Includes programs that are operated by divisions of the state or local government or prime sponsorship.

Of the twenty-seven community-based organizations in the sample, 77 percent experienced budget increases in the second year, while only 15 percent received less funds.[48]

Title I Program Expenditures

Manpower experts usually divide employment and training programs into five categories: classroom vocational training, on-the-job training, work experience programs, public service employment, and services to participants, such as assessment, counseling, and placement. A wide variety of programs fall within each category: a work experience program may involve part-time employment for high-school students or full-time work for adults in conjunction with classroom education. Nevertheless, the concepts are useful for understanding the different approaches for helping people get jobs. Prime sponsors were free to alter the mixture of employment and training programs that existed in their communities prior to the law's enactment. And, in some prime sponsorships, local officials were responsible for creating the mixture since their communities had never received employment and training funds.

Data reporting national trends in program expenditures reveal moderate differences between the categorical period and CETA. Classroom training programs dropped from 42 percent of the total allocation of manpower dollars in the last categorical year to 32 percent in the first year of CETA. On-the-job training programs also declined from 18 percent in fiscal year 1974 to 8 percent in fiscal year 1975.[49] Corresponding increases occurred in work experience programs and public service employment programs funded through the block grant Title I. Congress had permitted the use of Title I monies for public service employment programs, and, despite substantial increases in other public service employment programs, prime sponsors nearly doubled expenditures on Title I between fiscal years 1975 and 1976. By fiscal year 1977 more money was once again spent on classroom and on-the-job training programs, but expenditures were still shy of pre-CETA levels.

Explaining Program Design and Expenditure Decisions: The Model Applied

The evidence comparing the CETA period with categorical period indicates that moderate changes in methods of program delivery were accomplished, but large-scale reforms were not implemented. Categorical program operators, with the exception of the state employment service, fared well under CETA, spending about the same proportion of funds as before. Programs that provide direct employment, Title I-funded public service employment and work experience, found favor with CETA administrators and thus received increasing shares of CETA funds.

Policy Standards and Resources. The statute was vague about the who, what, when, and how of program design and expenditure decisions. Legislative framers of CETA avoided specifying how much money should be spent on what kinds of employment and training programs and who should run them. The policy standards set very wide boundaries within which state and local officials could implement their programs.

The resources provided by CETA, however, inhibited reforms at the local level in two senses. First, the resources provided through Title I were inadequate to foster innovation because they were spread thinly among the areas receiving funding. Many cities and counties were given programs to administer, after the funds coming into their communities had already been reduced. This made decisions to launch new programs politically more difficult because it meant that they would have to be funded from resources gained by eliminating an ongoing contract. Second, the huge increase of public service employment funds created a management problem that diverted national and local energies away from Title I planning and reform. As one senior Department of Labor official recalled, "Public Service Employment became synonymous with CETA and we forgot about Title I, which really is the guts of the program."

National Policy Environment. The national policy environment had little effect on program design and expenditures, but a few points are worth noting. Various groups at the national level pressured the Department of Labor to intervene in local program choices. National representatives of the categorical program operators sought Labor's protection. Predictably, prime sponsor representatives demanded freedom from federal interference. Overall, the department's influence, though moderate, tended to reinforce the status quo. For example, the state-run and federally financed state employment services received strong backing from DOL and probably would have lost more funds without it.

The Department of Labor certainly was not aggressive in promoting change and reform in local CETA programs,[50] but the growth of Title I public service employment programs and work experience programs raised enough concern in Labor that it finally issued regulations cautioning local governments not to put excessive amounts of their funds into such programs.[51] Ironically, the next year Congress practically guaranteed larger expenditures on work experience programs when it passed the Youth Employment Act. In general, the ineffectual federal role stemmed from the uncertain mandate in the statute, a lack of knowledge about what kinds of reform to promote, and the weakness of federal bureaucrats relative to elected officials.

The Local Policy Environment. Several elements of the local policy environment were influential in determining the nature of program design and expenditures in CETA.

1. The capability of agencies responsible for implementing CETA at the local level was severely taxed because most local staffs lacked training or experience in how to operate employment and training programs. Without a clear understanding of alternatives, this often led them simply to continue the previous arrangement of manpower programs. When the public service employment programs doubled only six months after the program started, local agencies that were already experiencing problems with CETA assumed an even more demanding task. Frequently the staff had no time or energy left for initiating reforms in the Title I delivery system.[52]

2. Local *interest group politics* also helped dampen the climate for reforming CETA programs. According to the Ohio State University study of CETA, "It is a well established fact that the selection of service deliverers in the first few years of CETA often represented highly political choices. . . . When scarce resources are to be divided, choices based partially on political considerations are virtually inevitable."[53] Such politically based decisions by elected officials usually led to the continued funding of powerful agencies in the community and the elimination of those agencies without a base of political support, such as the state employment service. Since elected officials were unable or unwilling to bring about significant

change in the roster of agencies running employment and training programs, they were also often unable to bring about substantial reform in the methods of program delivery.

3. The *attitudes of elected officials and their staffs* toward manpower reform and the efficacy of specific manpower programs had a strong influence on the degree and nature of change in local programs. For example, elected officials who believed that on-the-job training programs in the private sector provided the best approach to improving the employability of the disadvantaged funneled larger portions of their funds into those programs. Other officials preferred public service employment programs because they offered full-time work experience and helped get people immediately back to work. Whatever view officials took toward manpower programs, it usually made its way into program expenditure decisions. Because knowledge about which programs provided the most effective outcomes was limited, opinions of staff and officials were at first largely based on their perceptions and prejudices. In subsequent years, however, a few prime sponsors developed systematic evaluations and used them to guide their program decisions.

A staff's evaluation of its own ability to effect change as well as its worries about elected officials who might intervene on behalf of disaffected constituencies helped form its attitude toward CETA. According to one CETA planner in a large midwestern city, "Political agendas—hidden agendas—held by the mayor and his staff dominate decision making. If you make a move, you may have to take the heat." Of course, political officials not only prevented change; significant reform was observed in communities where the chief elected official encouraged and supported staff efforts to improve methods of program delivery.[54]

4. Finally, *local economic conditions* were a moderate constraint on program design and expenditure decisions. Though analysts have frequently argued that changes in local economic conditions can and should shape agency choices about which employment and training programs they run, the National Academy of Sciences and the Ohio State University studies found no evidence supporting this claim. The National Academy of Sciences observed similar levels of expenditures for public service employment, on-the-job training, work experience, and classroom training—the four major types of manpower programs—in communities with high, moderate, and low levels of unemployment.[55] According to the Ohio State researchers, there were very weak relationships between unemployment rates and decisions about how much money would be spent on different types of manpower programs.[56] Nevertheless, these analysts reported, some prime sponsors reacted to the rising unemployment rate by spending more money on programs that seemed to offer more immediate relief, namely, work experience and public service employment programs.[57]

Summary

National and local manpower professionals overwhelmingly desired manpower reform and hoped that CETA would foster change, but constraints imposed by political, agency, and economic features of the local policy environment frequently combined to inhibit innovations. The national policy environment did not have much influence on the substance of local CETA programs, but the Department of Labor occasionally intervened to support the existing structure of agencies and programs. Though the policy standards were unimportant in accounting for program performance because they were so broad, the growth in program resources in the public service employment programs authorized by Congress significantly inhibited reform under the Title I block grant programs.

**What Is the Nature of Public Service
Employment Programs?**

Up to this point, discussion of CETA has focused on its Title I programs, where state and local officials had wide discretion to formulate strategies for assisting the unemployed. Now the analysis shifts to CETA's public service employment programs funded under Titles II and VI. Here the statute is somewhat more specific about what state and local governments should do with their funds. Although the legislation permitted prime sponsors to use public service employment funds on training programs, 97 percent of the funds were in fact spent on public sector jobs.[58] But prime sponsors still had important choices to make, such as what kinds of agencies would recieve the public service employment money and what kinds of services they would provide. Table 3-4 helps put the size of public service employment programs into perspective. It displays the functional use of all employment and training programs from fiscal year 1975 to fiscal year 1978. It shows that PSE programs, which initially consumed 30 percent of the total CETA budget, doubled in size to 60 percent four years later. This section briefly considers how local governments used their public service employment funds.

The Distribution of PSE Jobs

Prime sponsors can allocate CETA-funded public service employment jobs to several types of organizations: agencies within city or county government; agencies in subordinate governments, such as townships, boroughs and villages; state agencies with facilities in the area; special purpose quasi-

Table 3-4
CETA Program Expenditures by Activity for Fiscal Years 1975-1979
(in millions of dollars and percent)

Program Activity	1975		1976		1977		1978		1979[a]	
	Amount	Percent	Amount	Percent	Amount	Percent	Amount	Percent	Amount	Percent
Training										
OJT[b]	118	3.9	272	5.2	399.2	5.7	398.9	4.1	675.3[c]	5.8
Classroom	634	20.7	866	16.6	966.4	16.4	1,249.2	12.9	1,457.8	12.4
Training	752	24.6	1,138	21.8	1,305.6	22.1	1,648.1	17.0	2,133.1	18.2
Work experience	1,355	44.4	1,491	28.5	1,494.8	25.3	2,023.2	20.9	3,097.3[d]	26.4
Public service employment	900	29.5	2,425	46.4	2,938.2	49.7	5,803.2	60.0	6,262.0	53.4
Other	47	1.5	173	3.3	170.4	2.9	201.7[e]	2.1	239.7	2.0
Total	3,054.0	100.0	5,227.0	100.0	5,909.0	100.0	9,676.2	100.0	11,732.1	100.0

Source: U.S., Congress, Congressional Budget Office, *CETA Reauthorization Issues* (Washington, D.C.: Government Printing Office, 1978), table 1, p. 5.
aAdministration estimate.
bOn-the-job training.
cIncludes estimated expenditure on the Private Sector Initiative Program.
dIncludes youth programs.
eIncludes $5 million Disabled Veterans Outreach Program.

governmental agencies such as boards of education or water authorities; and private, nonprofit agencies, such as a local hospital or boys club. Aside from decisions about which individuals will receive public service jobs, the distribution of PSE jobs to agencies is one of the most important choices that prime sponsors have to make under CETA.

Evidence from various studies of the distribution outcomes shows that local officials usually chose to put most PSE jobs in their own government's agencies. For example, in fiscal year 1976 only 3 percent of the public service jobs went to organizations outside the prime sponsor's agencies in cities under extreme fiscal pressure, only 18 percent were allocated outside the jurisdiction's agencies in cities under moderate fiscal pressure, and 33 percent were given to outside agencies in those experiencing little or no financial difficulties.[59]

Congress revised the public service employment programs in late 1976 in order to encourage prime sponsors to put more emphasis on funding PSE jobs in nonprofit agencies and, at the same time, doubled the available resources. A Brookings Institution evaluation of the way forty-two jurisdictions distributed jobs under the revised PSE program showed that 66 percent of the jobs went to agencies in those jurisdictions' governments. The rest were allocated to private nonprofit agencies (15 percent), local schools (8 percent), subordinate local governments (7 percent), and state agencies (4 percent).[60]

The Brookings analysis also categorized the functions performed by the public service employees. In sample jurisdictions, nearly half of the PSE participants engaged in "primary services" such as law enforcement, public works, utilities, sanitation, and administration. Only one-fifth of the participants were involved in social and cultural service jobs.[61] Moreover, the vast majority of primary service jobs were located in the city and county government agencies; the bulk of the cultural and social service positions, on the other hand, were found in private and nonprofit organizations.[62]

Donald Baumer's in-depth examination of PSE job distribution sheds light on the range of possible outcomes. During the two-year period of his study, three of the five cities and counties committed up to 100 percent of their PSE funds to their own agencies, while another city consistently used less than 50 percent of CETA-PSE funds for itself.[63]

The preceding discussion raises the issue of "substitution," or the extent to which local governments used federal funds in the public service employment program as a replacement for locally raised revenues. Substitution can take many forms. The most obvious one is the practice of using CETA funds to rehire laid-off city or county workers who were dismissed intentionally for this purpose. Rehiring people with CETA funds when a local government is forced to lay off people because of a genuine fiscal crisis is permitted under CETA. But there are many more subtle forms of substitution, such as "slotting CETA workers into existing vacancies or using them to meet expansion needs where such jobs would have otherwise been filled from local resources."[64] Obviously an accurate assessment of substitution is extremely difficult because it requires the analysts to determine what a city or county would have done without CETA funds. Using data gathered by experienced field researchers in over forty communities, the Brookings Institution's analysis of the public service employment expansion programs estimated substitution to be around 16 percent.[65] But other analysts, using methods based on statistical projections, estimated that the substitution of federal funds for local funds under PSE programs was 50 percent or more.[66]

Explaining the Distribution of PSE Jobs: The Model Applied

The analysis of public service employment programs revealed the tendency of local governments to allocate federally funded jobs to their own agencies, especially during the initial years of the CETA program. Most of the PSE jobs within local government were in primary governmental functions, such as public safety and sanitation.

Policy Standards and Resources. The original legislation authorizing CETA's public service employment programs did not specify which types of agencies should receive the jobs or what those agencies should use the money for. In contrast, the restructured public service employment program enacted by Congress in late 1976 mandated the creation of public service projects staffed by long-term unemployed and low-income people and established, as a goal, that one-third of all PSE jobs should be allocated to private nonprofit agencies. The revised law probably affected the distribution of PSE jobs, but that is not entirely clear. By the time the law passed Congress, many state and local governments had already reached a "PSE saturation point." In other words, they had already absorbed as many PSE workers as they could into their own agencies; additional money provided by the statute had to be given to organizations outside city and county government. Consequently, the increased proportion of CETA-PSE jobs in private, nonprofit agencies after 1976 may have been caused by the saturation effect rather than the target goal established by Congress.

The National Policy Environment. Overall, the Department of Labor's influence over public service job distribution was insignificant, according to the Ohio State University's study of seventeen Ohio prime sponsorships.[67]

Labor's concerted push to spend PSE funds rapidly may have indirectly shaped the nature of PSE outcomes, however, as it takes less staff time to design PSE jobs within the city or county government departments than for external organizations.[68]

The Local Policy Environment. Two features of the local policy environment helped determine how PSE funds would be used.

1. As noted earlier, political officials played central roles in making decisions about public service employment funds, but whether large numbers of PSE jobs were retained by the local government agencies depended on the attitudes of those officials toward the program. Some elected officials saw advantages to providing local governmental services with federally funded PSE workers. Others eschewed the PSE jobs and doled them out to nonprofit organizations because they feared being held accountable by disgruntled employees they would inevitably have to lay off when the federal funds dried up.[69]

2. Several evaluations of the public service employment programs show that cities and counties experiencing fiscal problems put higher proportions of PSE jobs in their own agencies than did those without such problems.[70] Fiscal problems made many officials overlook any reservations they might have had about becoming dependent on a federally funded PSE work force. Moreover, the Brookings study concluded that fiscally "distressed governments are much more likely to use PSE positions for primary services than for other kinds of activities."[71]

Who Benefits from CETA Jobs and Training?

Framers of the original CETA legislation debated about the characteristics of intended beneficiaries and about how much latitude local political officials should have to make enrollment decisions. Those opposed to broad eligibility criteria charged that many mayors, governors, and county officials remained insensitive to the plight of the disadvantaged because they did not draw political support from them. Those in favor countered that elected officials should be empowered to determine local needs and establish priorities for those who should participate in CETA programs.

CETA articulated broad national goals for serving low-income people and those most in need of employment and training services but left federal, state, and local implementors to decide the specific characteristics of program participants. In order to assess CETA's performance one needs to know what share of its resources were actually received by the poor, minorities, and other exigent groups. Using information from the Department of Labor and from studies of state and local prime sponsors, the following section describes the characteristics of people who participated in CETA Title I and public service employment programs and then compares them with participants in the earlier categorical programs. The nature of CETA's direct benefits—enrollment in a training program or placement in a federally funded public service job—rather than its impact on people's long-term employment or earnings potential is considered here.[72]

Title I Enrollment

Table 3-5 summarizes the characteristics of Title I participants during CETA's first four years and compares them with the characteristics of people who participated in similar categorical manpower programs in fiscal year 1974—the last year of federal control over the programs. According to the comparative data, enrollment of nonwhites, the poor, and people under

Table 3-5

Characteristics of CETA, Title I Participants, Compared with Those Participating in Categorical Programs for Fiscal Years 1974-1978
(in percent)

Participant Characteristics	Categorical Programs (FY 1974)[a]	CETA Title I Programs[b]				
		12/74	6/75	9/76	9/77	9/78
Females	42	49	45	46	48	51
Nonwhite	46	46	44	45	42	40
Under 22 years of age	63	65	62	57	52	49
With 12 or more years of education	34	34	39	46	50	52
Economically disadvantaged[c]	87	81	78	78	78	79

Sources: Categorical Data from U.S., Department of Labor, Employment and Training Administration, *Employment and Training Report of the President* (Washington, D.C.: Government Printing Office, 1976), p. 100. Data on the CETA period from Quarterly Summaries of Participant Characteristics supplied by the Employment and Training Administration.

[a]Includes programs funded under the Economic Opportunity Act and the Manpower Development and Training Act, such as the Neighborhood Youth Corps, Operational Mainstream, Skills Training, Job Opportunities in the Business Sector, and the Jobs Optional Program.

[b]The rationale for the choice of dates is as follows: data on the categorical period represent the federally managed period. December 1974 is the earliest date for which reliable data are available: June 1975, the first full year of CETA; September 1976, the second full year of CETA—reflecting a change in the federal fiscal year; September 1977 and 1978, the third and fourth full years of CETA.

[c]A person living in a family with less than the poverty income or receiving cash welfare assistance.

the age of twenty-two declined noticeably under CETA; but service to women and those with twelve or more years of education increased.

Enrollment *during* the CETA era followed this same general pattern. The percentage of economically disadvantaged participants decreased slightly overall, reaching a low point in June 1975 and increasing slightly by September 1978; but the poor still account for more than three-fourths of all participants. Enrollment of nonwhites and those under age twenty-two has fallen as well. Service to people with at least a high-school education has risen sharply, however, and participation by women increased after an initial decline.

Public Service Employment Program Participants

The original eligibility standards for the two public service employment programs were different. Public service employment under Title II was intended for the structurally unemployed who resided in areas with an unemployment rate of at least 6.5 percent. Title VI was aimed at people affected by the recession of late 1974. In fact, prime sponsors almost always jointly administered the two programs, so that it was virtually impossible to detect much differences between the participants or the programs. And, at one point, the Department of Labor temporarily eliminated any distinction between the two titles by allowing the free transfer of Title VI participants to Title II, and vice versa. Therefore, the following analysis combines Titles II and VI through fiscal year 1976. In fiscal year 1977, major revisions in Title VI entrance requirements were implemented in May of 1977. Consequently, data on the two titles for fiscal years 1977 and 1978 are reported separately.

Table 3-6 summarizes national aggregate information on enrollment in CETA's Title II and Title VI and compares it with that on enrollments in the pre-CETA Public Employment Program, which was authorized by the Emergency Employment Act. In contrast to Title I, CETA's PSE programs enrolled *more* economically disadvantaged participants than did the pre-CETA program. Nonwhite enrollment in PSE declined more significantly than in Title I programs, however, dropping 11 percent initially and remaining below categorical levels. The education and age levels of participants were stable between categorical programs and CETA's PSE programs, but women received more PSE jobs under CETA than before.

PSE enrollment trends *during* the CETA years show that service to the economically disadvantaged increased dramatically in fiscal years 1977 and 1978; minority enrollments increased slightly; age and educational backgrounds of participants remained stable, with roughly three-fourths of all

Table 3-6

Characteristics of CETA, Public Service Employment Participants, Compared
with Those Participating in Categorical Programs for Fiscal Years 1972-1978
(in percent)

Participant Characteristics	Categorical[a] Programs (FY 72 & 73)	CETA Titles II and VI[b]					
				9/77		9/78	
		6/75	9/76	II	VI	II	VI
Females	28	32	36	40	36	45	38
Nonwhite	40	29	33	28	34	28	33
22-44 years of age	66	64	64	65	65	65	65
With 12 or more years of education	74	74	75	78	73	80	72
Economically disadvantaged	38	44	44	48	66	62	81

Sources: See table 3-5.

[a]Includes figures from the Public Employment Program authorized by the Emergency Employment Act. The principal years of this program's operation were 1972 and 1973.

[b]The dates represent cumulative reports for fiscal years 1975, 1976, 1977, and 1978. Titles II and VI are separated in the data reported for fiscal years 1977 and 1978 because the eligibility requirements for Title VI were revised in the middle of fiscal year 1977, thus making the programs very different in their intended target population.

enrollees having at least a high-school-level education; and the percentage of women enrolled in the programs increased.

Title I and PSE Programs Compared

Significant differences among people enrolled in the divergent CETA programs are revealed by comparing the information in tables 3-5 and 3-6. People in Title I employment and training programs differ markedly from those hired in Titles II and VI public service jobs up through September 1977. Title I enrollees were much more likely to be economically disadvantaged, nonwhite, less well educated, female, and younger than PSE participants. By September 1978, after the new eligibility rules were fully instituted, Title VI participants were composed of the same percentage of poor people as Title I clients, but Title VI PSE participants were older as a group and much more likely to have had more formal education.

The implications of these distinctions between Title I and PSE are important for understanding who benefits from CETA. PSE programs were more costly per person than the average Title I program and typically provided more tangible rewards. A public service employment program gave people jobs paying approximately $8,000 per year on the average, whereas

Title I programs usually placed people in training schools with a small stipend or enrolled them in part-time work experience jobs at the minimum wage. In short, the more direct and costly benefits were distributed to a relatively more advantaged group of people, namely, those who were more competitive in the labor market to start with because of their educational superiority or more extensive work histories. Significantly, as noted above in table 3-4, the majority of CETA's funds went to public service employment programs.

Explaining Who Benefits: The Model Applied

A radical shift in enrollment patterns from pre-CETA to CETA did not materialize. The poor got less from Title I, but more from CETA's PSE programs than they received under federally managed categorical manpower programs. Enrollment of nonwhites declined in both Title I and PSE, and CETA enrollees were older and better educated than those involved during the categorical era. Sharp increases in Title VI's enrollment of the poor occurred in late 1977 and continued throughout 1978.

Policy Standards and Resources. Three characteristics of CETA help explain its distribution of benefits.

1. CETA's allocation formula created a flow of manpower dollars into suburban areas and away from central cities; as a result, CETA's available clientele is less poor and more white than were participants in the categorical programs, which were often restricted to serving people residing in the inner city.[73] The precise extent to which the increased money for the suburbs contributed to altered enrollment outcomes is not known; however, research on thirty-two state and local governments by Donald Baumer, Mary Marvel, and myself, a team of researchers from the Ohio State CETA study, strongly suggests that the allocation formula did not account for all the observed changes. During the CETA years, a number of prime sponsors in the three-year study reduced enrollment of the poor and other groups from the levels they had received during the categorical era, despite the fact that the geographical areas the prime sponsors served were identical.[74]

2. The original CETA entrance requirements were quite broad, especially in Title I, in which those unemployed for only seven days prior to enrollment were eligible. Requirements for Title I and PSE expanded the pool of individuals seeking manpower services. Over time, however, eligibility standards became more restrictive under Title VI PSE. For example, the length of required unemployment was one week for Title I, thirty days for Title II and the original Title VI program, and fifteen of the previous twenty weeks for the revised Title VI program. Only the revised

Title VI required a joint unemployment and poverty test for admission to its program. In order to get a Title VI PSE job, after the late 1976 amendment, one had to be *both* poor and unemployed for a substantial period of time. Sharp increases in enrollment of the poor during 1978 can be attributed in large part to the new Title VI statutory requirements.

A study by William Barnes, conducted under the auspices of the National Commission for Manpower Policy, estimates that, because of the size and diversity of the CETA-eligible population, state and local government officials had enormous discretion in selecting people to participate in CETA.[75] Barnes also points out that populations eligible for CETA's separate programs vary greatly in size: "Over the course of one year 26.7 million people are eligible for Title I; 12.2 million for Title II; 18.2 million for all provisions of Title VI; and 6.9 million for Title VIb (the PSE-Projects program)."[76] Considering that in fiscal year 1977 Title I enrolled 1,416,000, Title II employed 353,000 people, and Title VI provided 593,000 jobs, it is clear that prime sponsors chose a small percentage of the many people who were eligible.[77] For instance, in any given year, 30 percent of the work force of the United States between the ages of eighteen and sixty-five were eligible for Title I programs. In contrast, those eligible for the revised Title VI PSE program constitute about 8 percent of the eighteen to sixty-five work force.[78]

3. Finally, the goals of various CETA programs frequently clashed with one another and did not reflect the announced differences between the three titles. Title I, which was supposed to be reserved for the low-income and chronically unemployed, had the largest eligible population, 61 percent of which had completed high school. Title II, intended for the structurally unemployed, the Title VI, designed to counteract "emergency unemployment" during a recession, had almost identical entrance standards. Fifty percent of those qualifying for the most restrictive CETA program, the Title VI Project PSE program, were high-school graduates; nearly 20 percent had completed more than a year of college.[79] The messages contained in the statute were ambiguous and inconsistent with the rhetoric claiming that employment and training programs should be for those "most in need" of assistance.

The National Policy Environment. In general, policies of the Department of Labor and actions by its regional offices during the early years of CETA had a less direct impact on benefit distribution than did local decisions and conditions. Ohio State University researchers found only one city out of seventeen in which Labor's representative influenced the selection of clients for the local CETA program.[80] The Department of Labor simply did not concentrate its oversight activities on benefit distribution in CETA; however, its policies occasionally influenced enrollment patterns through seemingly unrelated decisions. During CETA's first two years, DOL placed legitimate, but perhaps excessive, stress on rapid expenditures, as noted above. Prime sponsors often responded to this directive by committing high proportions of funds to programs that could be quickly implemented. The unintended consequence was to push more money into PSE programs, curtailing opportunities for the less job-ready disadvantaged applicants.[81]

The department's firmer posture toward program enrollments in 1977 and 1978 came about after it received complaints from the Congress and various interest groups. But the most important element in the national policy environment was enactment of restrictive legislation, with much more specific goals for benefit distribution, in the PSE extension program and the Youth Employment and Demonstration Projects Act. Both targeted resources to a more narrow group of long-term unemployed and low-income people.

The Local Policy Environment. Three features of the local policy environment are significant in accounting for CETA's distribution of benefits.

1. The *economic and social characteristics* of a jurisdiction affected the characteristics of its potential CETA applicants. Some analysts speculated that changes in enrollment patterns over time and variation among prime sponsorships could be caused by changes *and* differences in the composition of the prime sponsor's community. Several analyses addressing the relationship between estimated need and CETA enrollments, however, undermine the claim that economic and social conditions dictate enrollment patterns.

Analysts from the Ohio State University study compared the state employment service's estimated characteristics of potential applicants with actual enrollment patterns in twenty-four local government prime sponsorships. These data reveal that one-third of the prime sponsors served a lower percentage of women under Title I than was present in the estimated eligible population; however, enrollment of the poor and nonwhites fell below estimated need in only one case. Enrollment of women and the poor in public service employment jobs was frequently below estimated proportions of these groups in the jurisdictions. Fourteen of the twenty-four prime sponsors underserved the economically disadvantaged and sixteen of the twenty-four sites underserved women. Only five of the prime sponsors served a lower percentage of nonwhites than was present in the estimates.[82] Barnes's study comparing characteristics of those enrolled in CETA programs with those present in the eligible population for the nation as a whole reported similar findings.[83]

The National Academy of Sciences study compared the characteristics of CETA participants with the characteristics of people who were unemployed for fifteen weeks or more in fiscal year 1976. Blacks received much more service under CETA's Title I than their proportion in this measure of need; service to women matched the need for such service; and those with limited education, eight or fewer years, were substantially underserved.[84] Females and those lacking formal educational training were underserved in Titles II and VI public service employment programs, but blacks received somewhat more service than they needed as predicted by this measure.[85]

2. Local program funding decisions and the growth of public service employment programs affected participant enrollment patterns in two senses. First, because different types of employment and training programs demand different enrollee qualifications and preparation, the programs themselves indirectly determine the characteristics of people served by them. Classroom training and work experience programs usually require little of applicants because programs can be built around their needs. Public service employment and on-the-job training programs, however, depend on the requirements of the employer requesting a CETA worker. Such programs often create substantial barriers to the least qualified individuals. For example, an agency requesting a CETA-funded administrative assistant could specify that they need someone with a college degree and two years of office management experience.

Several studies examined the relationships between program type and participants. Though the results are not overwhelmingly clear, they indicate that program strategies selected by elected officials and staffs influenced the distribution of benefits. The impact of programmatic decisions was particularly strong where prime sponsors put large amounts of their Title I funds into public service employment jobs, because this boosted the qualifications that people needed to get into the program.[86]

Second, the selection of programs contractors influenced benefit distribution, because decisions about whom to enroll in CETA were often made by those agencies. At minimum, program contractors partially shaped the characteristics of people in CETA because of their physical locations and the agency's general reputation for dealing with various segments in the community. For example, some community organizations were associated with minority groups; others tended to deal more effectively with white applicants. Prime sponsor staffs and elected officials often based their choice of program contractors on the agency's history of working with groups that the prime sponsor wanted to serve.

The above discussion reported only marginal changes in the lineup of program deliverers between the categorical era and CETA. In many communities this fact probably helped preserve the status quo in benefit distribution. Because many of the same agencies handled program enrollment under CETA that had done it under the categorical period, participant service patterns were predictably similar. On the other hand, some prime sponsors centralized the decisions about who would be enrolled in CETA programs in order to assert the preferences of the staff and elected officials, thus making change in enrollment patterns possible.

3. The *attitudes of local actors* were also important in explaining who benefits from CETA. Local economic conditions, filtered through the perceptions and preferences of manpower actors, and decisions about program design indirectly represented the staff and elected officials' preferences. For instance, the assumption among many officials that the recession of 1974 altered the overall composition of people applying for CETA training and jobs influenced decisions about who should benefit from CETA. Declining percentages of low-income people in CETA corresponded to the opinion held by many state and local government officials that higher levels of unemployment reduced the proportion of low-income people in the applicant pool. Few prime sponsors analyzed the changes to determine what actually occurred.[87]

The preferences of local decision-makers about who should receive CETA services were frequently reflected in actual benefit distribution, according to a survey conducted by the Ohio State University CETA research group. Professional staff dominated Title I enrollment decisions in all but three of the thirty-two prime sponsors: there were clear relationships between the staff's preferences and enrollment levels of various groups. Public officials played a far more central role in PSE program choices. In twenty-three of thirty-two jurisdictions, political officials influenced public service employment outcomes. Moreover, PSE enrollment decisions were usually made by city or county department heads or aids of local elected officials. In general, low enrollments of poor prople were associated with highly involved political officials who generally had low commitments to serving the economically disadvantaged through public service employment. Equally important in PSE outcomes was the attitude of the manpower staff, because they too tended to favor far less service for the poor in PSE than in Title I programs.[88]

Active and influential manpower planning councils did not exercise much influence over the distribution of CETA benefits. Because the typical planning council was dominated by service providers and representatives of political jurisdictions, they concentrated on matters related to organizational survival rather than the status of low-income or minority clients. Occasionally, however, planning councils demanded programs for the economically disadvantaged; restrained elected officials from placing large amounts of funds into programs that would not serve the poor, such as Title I, public service employment; or advanced the cause of a constituency to the staff and elected officials. Of particular interest in the light of the findings on benefit distribution is the fact that unemployed women were poorly represented on the manpower planning council; as a group, women received the least benefits in relation to their proportion of the unemployed population. In contrast, minority groups, which have been better represented, continued to be reasonably effective in gaining services.[89]

Summary

Local economic conditions and the perception of their impact affected not only the types of people who sought CETA services but also decisions about who should receive them. But enrollment outcomes were not wholly determined by economic and demographic factors. The attitudes and actions of elected officials and their staffs regarding employment and training program design and about appropriate levels of service for certain groups played a critical role in shaping enrollment patterns. Indeed, prime sponsor staffs and elected officials in various communities reacted very differently to similar economic conditions. Finally, the statute and the initial actions of the Department of Labor, though less important than the local policy environment, accentuated trends toward reduced enrollment of the disadvantaged under CETA. Changes in law and department policy in the later years of CETA modified these trends. And CETA's 1978 reauthorization mandated national target groups for all CETA programs, thus restricting the scope of local discretion.

Notes

1. "CETA: Successful Job Program or Subsidy for Local Government?" *Congressional Quarterly Weekly Report* 36 (1978):799.

2. As quoted in Charles Culhane, "Revenue Sharing Shift Set for Worker Training Programs," *National Journal Reports* 6 (1974):52.

3. Representative David Obey (D.-Wis.) quoted in "Major CETA Jobs Program Extended through Fiscal '82," *Congressional Quarterly Weekly Report* 36 (1978):3185.

4. National Commission for Manpower Policy, *Job Creation through Public Service Employment, Volume II: Monitoring the Public Service Employment Program Report No. 6.* Prepared by Richard P. Nathan et al. (Washington, D.C.: Government Printing Office, 1978), p. 7 (hereafter NCMP, *Monitoring PSE*).

5. Sar A. Levitan, Garth Mangum, and Ray Marshall, *Human Resources and Labor Markets* (New York: Harper and Row, 1972), p. 299.

6. For fine histories of the categorical period see Garth Mangum, *MDTA: The Foundation of Federal Manpower Policy* (Baltimore: Johns Hopkins Press, 1968; and Stanley H. Ruttenberg and Jocelyn Gutchess, *Manpower Challenge of the 1970s* (Baltimore: Johns Hopkins Press, 1970).

7. Levitan, Mangum, and Marshall, *Human Resources and Labor Markets*, p. 259.

8. The best accounts of CETA's legislative history may be found in Roger H. Davidson, *The Politics of Comprehensive Manpower Legislation* (Baltimore: Johns Hopkins Press, 1972); and Sar A. Levitan and Joyce K. Zickler, *The Quest for a Workable Federal Manpower Partnership* (Cambridge, Mass.: Harvard Univ. Press, 1974).

9. As quoted in Davidson, *The Politics of Comprehensive Manpower Legislation,* p. 7.

10. Ibid., pp. 23-37.

11. Richard M. Nixon, "Veto Message," *Weekly Compilation of Presidential Documents* 6 (21 December 1970):1696.

12. Davidson, *The Politics of Comprehensive Manpower Legislation*, p. 91.

13. Richard M. Nixon, "Manpower Revenue Sharing Message," *Weekly Compilation of Presidential Documents* 7 (8 March 1971):419-422.

14. U.S., Executive Office of the President, Office of Management and Budget, *Budget of the United States Government, Fiscal Year 1974* (Washington, D.C.: Government Printing Office, 1973), p. 130.

15. U.S., Congress, House, Committee on Education and Labor, Select Subcommittee on Labor, *Comprehensive Manpower Act of 1973,* 93rd Cong., 2nd sess., 28-29 October 1973, p. 110.

16. For an excellent summary of CETA see Patrick O'Keefe, Robert Ainsworth, and Everett Crawford, "Overview of the Program," in *CETA: An Overview of the Issues*, Special Report No. 23 of the National Commission for Manpower Policy (Washington, D.C.: Government Printing Office, 1978), pp. 31-62.

17. NCMP, *Monitoring PSE*, p. 11.

18. See, for example, ibid., pp. 6-13, for a short history of public service employment programs.

19. U.S., Congressional Research Service, Library of Congress, "The Comprehensive Employment and Training Act of 1973, as Amended; a Brief Summary" (Washington, D.C.: House Document 5720 B, August 5, 1977), p. 13 (hereafter CRS, "CETA Legislative History").

20. NCMP, *Monitoring PSE*, pp. 12-13.

21. CRS, "CETA Legislative History," p. 1.

22. For a good summary of the changes made in the 1978 reauthorization of CETA see "Major CETA Jobs Program Extended through Fiscal '82," *Congressional Quarterly Weekly Report* 36 (1978):3184-3189.

23. National Research Council, "Early Perceptions of the Comprehensive Employment and Training Act," papers presented at the initial meeting of the Committee on Evaluation of Employment and Training Programs (Washington, D.C.: National Academy of Sciences, 1974), p. 3.

24. U.S., Congress, House, Committee on Education and Labor, Select Subcommittee on Labor, *Employment and Manpower Act of 1972,* 92nd Cong., 1st sess., pp. 997-998.

25. Ibid., pp. 1004-1005.

26. "The Comprehensive Employment and Training Act," Public Law 93-203.

27. See, for example, Randall B. Ripley et al., *The Implementation of CETA in Ohio,* R&D Monograph No. 44, Employment and Training Administration, U.S. Department of Labor (Washington, D.C.: Government Printing Office, 1977),pp. 5-12 (hereafter Ripley et al., *CETA in Ohio*); and William Mirengoff and Lester Rindler, *CETA: Manpower Programs under Local Control* (Washington, D.C.: National Academy of Sciences, 1978), pp. 50-60.

28. Ripley et al., *CETA in Ohio*, pp. 6-7; and, Mirengoff and Rindler, *CETA*, p. 51.

29. Ripley et al., *CETA in Ohio*, p. 7; and Mirengoff and Rindler, *CETA*, p. 52.

30. Ripley et al., *CETA in Ohio*, pp. 7-8.

31. Mirengoff and Rindler, *CETA*, p. 56.

32. Randall Ripley et al., *Progress Report, The Implementation of CETA in Ohio*, prepared for the Employment and Training Administration, U.S. Department of Labor, September 15, 1975, mimeo, p. 81.

33. Ripley et al., *CETA in Ohio*, pp. 59-60.

34. This section draws on my "Implementing CETA: The Federal Role," *Policy Analysis* 4 (1978):159-183.

35. James W. Singer, "Administration Adjusts Its Aim at Job Training Targets," *National Journal Reports* 9 (1977):680.

36. This section is based on research conducted by the author and cited in note 34.

37. Quotations from practitioners, unless otherwise noted, come from personal interviews conducted by the author. Respondents were guaranteed anonymity.

38. Carl E. Van Horn, "Intergovernmental Policy Implementation: The Comprehensive Employment and Training Act," Ph.D. Dissertation, Ohio State University, 1976, pp. 132-133.

39. Ibid., p. 133.

40. See, for example, Donald C. Baumer, "Implementing Public Service Employment," in Judith V. May and Aaron B. Wildavsky, eds., *The Policy Cycle* (Beverly Hills: Sage Publications, 1978), pp. 180, 182; and Mirengoff and Rindler, *CETA*, p. 52.

41. See Randall B. Ripley et al., *Area-Wide Planning in CETA: Final Progress Report*, prepared for the Employment and Training Administration, U.S. Department of Labor, February 28, 1979, mimeo.

42. Mirengoff and Rindler, *CETA*, p. 58.

43. Van Horn, "Implementing CETA," pp. 178-179.

44. U.S., Congress, Senate, Committee on Labor and Public Welfare, Subcommittee on Employment, Manpower, and Poverty, *Manpower Development and Training Legislation, 1970*, 91st Cong., 1st and 2nd sess., p. 103.

45. Mirengoff and Rindler, *CETA*, p. 138.

46. Randall B. Ripley et al., *CETA Prime Sponsor Management and Program Goal Achievement*, R&D Monograph No. 56, Employment and Training Administration, U.S. Department of Labor (Washington, D.C.: Government Printing Office, 1978), p. 7 (hereafter, Ripley et al., *CETA Management*.)

47. Mirengoff and Rindler, *CETA*, p. 140.

48. Ripley et al., *CETA in Ohio*, p. 21.

49. Observations about program expenditures in Title I are based on data compiled by Mirengoff and Rindler, *CETA*, p. 118. These data compare the categorical programs of fiscal year 1974 with similar programs under CETA in fiscal years 1975 through 1977.

50. Van Horn, "Implementing CETA," pp. 166-167.

51. Mirengoff and Rindler, *CETA*, p. 120.

52. Ripley et al., *CETA Management*, pp. 20-21.

53. Ibid., p. 27.

54. Ripley et al., *Area-Wide Planning in CETA, Third Progress Report*, Prepared for the Employment and Training Administration, U.S. Department of Labor, September 30, 1978, mimeo, pp. 2-34.

55. Mirengoff and Rindler, *CETA*, p. 120.

56. Ripley et al., *CETA Management*, pp. 21-24.

57. Donald C. Baumer, Carl E. Van Horn, and Mary K. Marvel, "Explaining Benefit Distribution in CETA Programs" *Journal of Human Resources* 14 (1979):189-190.

58. U.S., Congress, Congressional Budget Office, *CETA Reauthorization Issues* (Washington, D.C.: Government Printing Office, 1978), p. 88.

59. Mirengoff and Rindler, *CETA*, p. 165.

60. NCMP, *Monitoring PSE*, p. 84.

61. Ibid., p. 79.

62. Ibid., p. 83.

63. Baumer, "Implementing Public Service Employment," p. 181.

64. Mirengoff and Rindler, *CETA*, p. 189.

65. NCMP, *Monitoring PSE*, p. 67.

66. See, for example, George E. Johnson and James D. Tomola, "The Fiscal Substitution Effect of Alternative Approaches to Public Service Employment," *Journal of Human Resources* 12 (1977):3-26.

67. Ripley et al., *CETA Management*, p. 7.

68. Van Horn, "Implementing CETA," pp. 169-170.

69. Mirengoff and Rindler, *CETA*, p. 163; and NCMP, *Monitoring PSE*, p. 90.

70. Mirengoff and Rindler, *CETA*, p. 164; NCMP, *Monitoring PSE*, p. 88; and Baumer, "Implementing Public Service Employment," p. 180.

71. NCMP, *Monitoring PSE,* p. 88.

72. For a study that assesses the long-term impact of employment and training programs see C.R. Perry et al., *The Impact of Government Manpower Programs* (Philadelphia: Industrial Research Unit, The Wharton School, Univ. of Pennsylvania, 1975).

73. U.S., Advisory Commission on Intergovernmental Relations, *The Comprehensive Employment and Training Act: Early Readings from a Hybrid Block Grant* (Washington, D.C.: Government Printing Office, 1977), p. 39; and, Mirengoff and Rindler, *CETA*, pp. 206-207.

74. Baumer, Van Horn, and Marvel, "Explaining Benefit Distribution in CETA Programs," pp. 191-192.

75. William Barnes, "Target Groups," in *CETA: An Overview of the Issues*, Special Report No. 23. of the National Commission for Manpower Policy (Washington, D.C.: Government Printing Office, 1978), pp. 63-101.

76. Ibid., p. 74.

77. Mirengoff and Rindler, *CETA*, p. 200.

78. Barnes, "Target Groups," p. 74.

79. Ibid., pp. 75, 77.

80. Ripley et al., *CETA in Ohio*, pp. 7-8.

81. Van Horn, "Implementing CETA," pp. 164-165.

82. Baumer, Van Horn, and Marvel, "Explaining Benefit Distribution in CETA Programs," p. 183.

83. Barnes, "Target Groups," pp. 93.

84. Mirengoff and Rindler, *CETA*, p. 205.

85. Ibid., p. 215.

86. Ibid., p. 208; and Baumer, Van Horn, and Marvel, "Explaining Benefit Distribution in CETA Programs," pp. 187-188.

87. Baumer, Van Horn, and Marvel, "Explaining Benefit Distribution in CETA Programs," pp. 189-190.

88. Ibid., p. 190.

89. Ibid., p. 191.

4 Community Development Block Grants: Aid for Urban America

In August of 1974 President Gerald Ford signed the Housing and Community Development Act, an omnibus housing law that authorized housing subsidy programs, public housing construction, mortgage insurance, and rural housing. Its most important segment was Title I, the Community Development Block Grant (CDBG), which consolidated several grant-in-aid programs and authorized over $8 billion for local governments to establish "viable urban communities." The legislation was praised by congressional Democrats and Republicans and by the diverse interest groups who had participated in reforming federal community development programs.

Despite this chorus of commendation, CDBG had been the focus of intergovernmental discord throughout its formulation, and elements reflecting that discord were written into the law. President Ford's remarks at the signing ceremonies reflected the inherent tension between national goals and local priorities:

> This bill will help return power from the banks of the Potomac to the people in their own communities. Decisions will be made at the local level. . . . And responsibility for results will be placed squarely where it belongs—at the local level.
>
> I pledge that this Administration will administer the program in exactly this way. . . . At the same time, of course, we will not abdicate the Federal government's responsibility to oversee the way the taxpayers' money is used.[1]

Participants favoring reduced federal control over local programs in the debate over community development reform were pleased with the first part of the president's remarks; those who argued for continued federal oversight appreciated the important caveat he added.

The Community Development Act removed restrictive federal requirements, but federal oversight was written into the law. Ambiguity about the degree of federal control and direction versus local discretion persisted through the major reauthorization of CDBG in 1977. When the federal agency responsible for implementing the law, the Department of Housing and Urban Development (HUD), took a more assertive position on federal responsibilities in 1978, the Congress rewrote CDBG in order to prohibit HUD from "exerting greater influence over the spending of community development funds."[2] CDBG's legislative history will help to explain its complex and controversial evolution.

101

A Legislative History of CDBG

An array of schemes for revitalizing the nation's urban communities can be classified as community development programs. Federal lawmakers first employed the term "community development" in the Housing Act of 1949, when they asserted that the "general welfare and security of the nation . . . require housing production *and related community development* sufficient to remedy the serious housing shortage" caused by the postwar population boom (emphasis in original).[3] Early community development policy concentrated on physical redevelopment through such programs as slum clearance, but over the years the community development policy domain encompassed such diverse programs as demolition of dilapidated housing, education and social services for urban residents, and reform of local political organizations through citizen participation.[4]

The legislative history of CDBG, spanning a quarter of a century, is characterized by roughly four major periods. The first phase was marked by the development of several specific federal aid programs assisting cities in their community development efforts. In the late 1960s and early 1970s, the second period of CDBG's development, Congress, the executive branch, and interest groups attempted to restructure the nature and scope of community development programs. Their efforts climaxed with the authorization of CDBG in 1974. Three years later, CDBG was reauthorized with important revisions. The final period in CDBG's development occurred in 1978 when Congress restrained the Department of Housing and Urban Development from intervening in local government decisions about CDBG usage.

Between 1949 and the eventual enactment of CDBG, dozens of federal aid programs that could be classified under the general rubric of community development emerged in piecemeal fashion. Some of the most important ones are briefly discussed here.[5]

The Housing Act of 1949 authorized programs of urban redevelopment through land acquisition and clearance. The largest of all community development programs, it allocated over $9 billion during its twenty-five-year history for thousands of urban renewal projects. The concept of redevelopment contained in the original legislation was broadened by the Housing Act of 1954, which added housing *rehabilitation* as a community developmment strategy.

Title VIII of the Housing Act of 1961 provided over $600 million to purchase and improve land in urban communities for use as recreation areas and to preserve important historic buildings.

Title VII of the Housing Act of 1965 added grants for water and sewer facilities, expending nearly $1 billion through 1973. In the same bill, grants for the construction of neighborhood facilities such as daycare or health centers were also established, and hundreds of communities mounted projects costing over $250 million.

Title I of the Demonstration Cities and Metropolitan Development Act of 1966, commonly referred to as the Model Cities Program, departed from the bulldozer and public works strategies embodied in the previous legislation and emphasized instead the linkage between urban blight and the economic, political, and social problems of a city's population. Over 140 Model Cities were established and supported through grants for a host of services from job training to housing rehabilitation. Perhaps most important, Model Cities mandated extensive participation by the model neighborhood's residents in the development and administration of local programs. In seven years, the Model Cities program distributed over $2.25 billion.

Each categorical program that was created represented a different method of attempting to cope with the problems of urban America. Various definitions of the urban problem produced disparate strategies, methods of funding, and delivery systems. With over twelve agencies running nearly 200 separate programs with complicated regulations, multiple deadlines, and lengthy approval periods, the categorical community development programs were charitably described as fragmented and frequently vilified as an "administrative monster."[6] Nearly all urban experts blamed the patchwork of urban policies for causing excessive competition among communities, delays in funding, and distortion of local priorities.

Several attempts to improve the management of community development programs were made in the late 1960s and early 1970s. The Housing Act of 1968 authorized one of the first efforts to strengthen local planning for urban renewal projects. Called the Neighborhood Development program, it was supposed to foster comprehensive planning for urban renewal programs. It also introduced more flexibility into the funding of smaller-scale community development projects on an annual basis.

Two experiments initiated by the administration of Richard Nixon tested the concept of urban special revenue sharing—the idea that elected officials should shape community development priorities. The Planned Variations program, incorporated into Model Cities, gave local officials more power to establish local priorities for how federal funds would be applied. Because the Planned Variations approach provided for limited federal agency review and substantial involvment by local elected officials, it was an important forerunner of CDBG.[7] The Annual Arrangement program, also launched by the Department of Housing and Urban Development, promoted coordination of the disparate community development grant programs by local elected officials. Participation by mayors, however, varied widely, and legal restrictions on the use of federal grants made comprehensive planning extremely difficult.

President Nixon introduced legislative proposals for reform of community development programs in early 1971. Citing the shortcomings of the categorical aid system, he proposed consolidating several community development programs and decentralizing authority for their management to local elected officials. In a message on urban special revenue sharing, Nixon reviewed the deficiencies of the federal system:

> State and local officials are often forced to function as wards of the Federal Government. Often they are treated as children who are given a meager allowance, told precisely how to spend it, and then scolded for not being self-reliant enough to handle more responsibility. If we want State and local government to survive, then we must break into this vicious cycle.[8]

The administration's Urban Community Development Revenue Sharing bill consolidated four categorical programs, including urban renewal, Model Cities, neighborhood facilities grants, and rehabilitation housing loans.

Urban special revenue sharing did not get very far. Though the principal actors in the community development policy arena—key members of Congress, representatives of state and local governments, and housing program specialists—agreed that decategorization was desirable, the question of how much power should be devolved to local elected officials provoked sharp disagreement. Congressional Democrats, dissatisfied with President Nixon's proposal for limited federal review, passed legislation in 1971 and 1972 endorsing the block grant concept but inserting detailed application requirements and extensive federal monitoring.

Not deterred by the initial failure to obtain legislation favored by the administration, Republicans reintroduced urban special revenue sharing, known as the Better Communities bill, in 1973. The renamed bill was essentially the same as the original proposal, but more community development programs were folded in. Reflecting the positions Congress had almost endorsed in 1972, the new bill added urban counties as a category of grant recipients and inserted a provision guaranteeing continued benefits to cities already receiving funds.[9]

These conciliatory gestures by the administration were accompanied by hardnosed tactics designed to prod Congress into an acceptable compromise. The president announced that he would suspend funds for the seven categorical programs included in the Better Communities bill until reform legislation was enacted. Instead of producing a quick settlement, however, this grant-in-aid moratorium provoked lawsuits to reverse the decision and a House Joint Resolution authorizing funds for housing and urban development programs, thus counteracting the president's actions.[10]

The two pieces of legislation that were eventually molded into the Housing and Community Development Act were introduced in the House and Senate in 1973. The Senate bill consolidated several urban aid programs into a block grant but advocated detailed national goals. For example, the bill required that 80 percent of all funds be spent on the low- and moderate-income residents of each commuity and prohibited local officials from allocating more than 20 percent of their grant for social service programs.

The House bill, initially similar to the Senate version, was modified during negotiations with the administration.[11] The compromise bill required applications from communities but deleted the detailed line-by-line review characteristic of the categorical grants. HUD would be expected to approve local plans unless they were inconsistent with the needs of the community. According to a senior HUD official who helped negotiate the agreement with the House Subcommittee on Housing, the application requirement preserved latitude for local decision-makers "with a safety valve in the department in case some community gets blatantly out of line."[12] A minimal application process was favored by representatives of communities that had prospered under the categorical aid programs, which rewarded superior grantsmanship. They insisted, however, on less federal intervention.

After the Senate and House bills passed their respective chambers, disagreements were worked out in a conference committee. The prolonged deliberations by House and Senate conferees dwelt on the formula for distributing the funds to communities and the degree of federal control over program priorities. The Senate position, favoring guaranteed funding of those communities already involved in federally supported community development programs, was approved. But the rest of the bill reported out by the conference committee generally incorporated the positions of the administration-backed House bill.[13] For example, the Senate bill's ceiling on social service expenditures was dropped. Its specific low- and moderate-income requirement was replaced by general national goals directing priority to low- and moderate-income persons.

Title I of the Housing and Community Development Act eliminated several categorical grant-in-aid programs including urban renewal, Model Cities, water and sewer facilities grants, neighborhood facilities grants, and open space loans. Rehabilitation loans were to have been folded into CDBG, but Congress has maintained the program through separate appropriations. Congress authorized $8.6 billion for three years, with $2.5 billion for fiscal year 1975, $3 billion for fiscal year 1976, and $3.1 billion for fiscal year 1977.[14]

The law distributed funds to a variety of communities through different funding mechanisms.[15] Most of the block grant funds (80 percent) were reserved for metropolitan areas, including cities with populations over 50,000 and eligible urban counties—those with over 200,000 residents and authority to handle community development activities. A formula incorporating the number of overcrowded housing units, the total population, and the proportion of people below the poverty level, weighted double, was used to calculate each community's entitlement block grant. A hold-harmless provision, calculated from the average amount of categorical grant money received by a community over five years, insured that each community got funds roughly equivalent to its previous level. Over time, however, the hold-harmless status would be removed, and communities would receive their formula allocations. The remaining 20 percent of the CDBG allocation was meted out to nonmetropolitan communities through discretionary grants. Unlike the automatic entitlement grants for metropolitan areas, these grants were made on a competitive basis. But because the hold-harmless provision also applied to nonmetropolitan funds, it was not immediately a discretionary program. Table 4-1 gives detailed budget information on allocations to several categories of CDBG recipients from fiscal year 1975 to fiscal year 1978.

The Community Development Block Grant's primary objective, as stated in the statute, was the creation of "viable urban communities by providing decent housing and a suitable living environment for persons of low and moderate income" (Section 101 [c]).[16] Without mandating specific priorities, the law stated seven national objectives that communities should consider in designing community development programs, such as the elimination of slums and blight, conservation and expansion of the nation's housing stock, the improvement of community services, and the reduction of income group isolation. Most of the national objectives reiterate the federal goal of service to low- and moderate-income persons (Section 101 [c]). Thirteen eligible activities were also listed, concentrating on physical development and public works projects and deemphasizing social service approaches (Section 105).

Grant recipients were obliged to make a multitude of assurances to HUD in their applications. The most important ones were assurances that the grantee had given "maximum feasible priority" to low- or moderate-income families, provided for public hearings and adequate opportunity for citizen participation, and submitted a Housing Assistance Plan (HAP). The HAP had to analyze the conditions of the community's housing stock and evaluate the needs of its low-income residents or those expected to reside there as a result of current or future employment opportunities. Communities also were required to state goals for the number of low-income housing units to be constructed, and the number of low-income people to be assisted, and to state the location of low-income housing units in the community.

Although communities submitted elaborate plans and assurances as part of their CDBG applications, the federal administering agency, HUD, could veto plans within seventy-five days, but only if the plans were plainly inconsistent with available facts, clearly not permissible under the act, or

Table 4-1
CDBG Appropriations for Fiscal Years 1975-1978 by Recipient Type
(in millions of dollars)

	Number of Units to Which Allocation Was Made				Dollar Amount Allocated			
	1975	*1976*	*1977*	*1978*	*1975*	*1976*	*1977*	*1978*
U.S. total appropriation[a]					$2,500,000	$2,752,000	$3,148,000	$3,500,000
Metropolitan Areas (SMSAs)					2,003,572	2,179,600	2,519,229	2,809,230
Metro cities	521	522	537	559	1,657,189	1,718,175	1,916,795	2,161,100
Urban counties	73	75	78	81	119,176	208,563	328,674	372,222
Small hold harmless units of government	299	301	305	268	172,565	170,933	173,760	105,165
Discretionary balance funds (SMSAs) or (states & P.R.)					54,642	81,929	100,000	170,743
Nonmetropolitan Areas					469,494	519,400	577,808	596,270
Small hold harmless units of government	449	450	443	436	269,799	265,397	254,890	159,286
Discretionary balance funds (states & P.R.)					199,695	254,003	322,918	436,984
Secretary's Discretionary Fund	—	—	—	—	26,934	53,000	50,963	94,500
Total units of Government	1,342	1,348	1,363	1,344				

Source: U.S., Department of Housing and Urban Development, *Community Development Block Grants, Directory of Allocations for FY '78* (Washington, D.C.: Government Printing Office, 1978), p. vii.

[a]Not including Urgent Needs Funds or Urban Development Action Grants.

plainly inappropriate to meeting local needs (Section 104 [c]). The law also directed HUD to conduct a detailed evaluation of each grant recipient, after the programs were already under way.

Three years after the original act took effect, and after months of intense legislative debate and manuevering, the Community Development Block Grant was reauthorized for another three years at a total funding level of $12.4 billion. Several significant changes occurred in the law.[17]

First, the new act established two allocation formulas for distributing CDBG money. The General Accounting Office, the Brookings Institution, and various interest groups had been highly critical of the 1974 formula's impact on older cities with declining populations.[18] Because the 1974 formula rewarded cities with growing populations, communities in the South and West gained substantially more community development funds. The revised law distributed grants to entitlement communities—those mandated by statute to receive funding—through the formula that gave them the most money. The 1974 formula, based on population, overcrowded housing units, and families in poverty, was supplemented with a new formula using age of housing, number of poor families, and growth lag. The "age of housing stock" indicator, based on the number of housing units built in 1939 or before, was a proxy for community needs created by the aging of its housing and not a direct measure of housing quality. The extent to which a community had fallen behind the average growth rate since 1960 constituted the "growth lag" measure. In general, the new formula benefited cities of the Northeast and Middlewest.[19]

Second, the new law authorized an Urban Development Action Grant program for annually spending $400 million on economic development activities in the nation's most severely depressed cities. Over the three-year period funds were to be distributed at HUD's discretion, using criteria suggested by Congress.

Third, although the Congress rejected Senate proposals to target funds to lower-income groups, the law did place somewhat stronger emphasis on lower-income families. At the same time, however, the statute also permitted activities that would directly benefit higher-income groups. This change in the law revisited the dispute between Senate and House members, during the 1974 authorization, over the question of who should benefit from CDBG funds.

Finally, the 1977 revisions encouraged communities to increase opportunities for citizen participation by requiring written plans describing efforts to foster citizen involvement and by giving citizens the right to "comment on CDBG program performance."[20]

The long-standing disagreement over the extent to which CDBG should benefit low- and moderate-income groups resurfaced almost as soon as the

1977 law passed Congress. HUD proposed regulations requiring communities to spend at least 75 percent of their CDBG funds on low- and moderate-income persons.[21] Secretary Patricia Harris commented, "The regulations . . . send a clear message to our constituents. HUD is targeting its funds more carefully to the needs of the poor."[22]

Because the 1977 legislation did *not* reserve a specific proportion of funds for low- and moderate-income people, reactions from many members of Congress and national interest groups representing local governments were sharply critical.[23] In order to insure that HUD would not reject a community's CDBG application for not complying with HUD's definition of adequate service to lower-income groups, Congress prohibited HUD from this practice in its 1978 fiscal year authorization. Congress also insisted that HUD submit proposed regulations to Congress for their review prior to taking any action.[24]

Summary

CDBG has been engulfed in controversy from the beginning because it raised fundamental questions about the distribution of federal funds. Most vexing were whether its funding formula measured genuine need and which community development strategies provided the most benefit to the low-and moderate-income families that make up a large segment of the nation's central cities. Throughout CDBG's legislative history the federal government's obligation to promote national objectives and the value of maintaining local decision-making flexibility have been in constant conflict. The law's modifications in 1977 and 1978 indicate that a majority in Congress preferred ambiguity. Consequently, central questions remained to be addressed during the implementation process by federal agencies and by local actors.

Implementing CDBG: What Happened and Why?

The analysis of CDBG's performance is broken down into three segments focusing on the role of elected officials, citizen participation, and the federal government; community development program strategies; and the distribution of program benefits. Because evidence on the impact of legislative revisions made in the 1977 law is very limited, primary attention is paid to the implementation of the original law. Each section considers in more detail the legislation's goals, information on program performance, and explanations for the observed outcomes.

Who Governs? The Role of Elected Officials, Citizens, and the Federal Government

The legislative history of the Community Development Act contained a drawn-out debate over the distribution of authority among levels of government to carry out the law: participants argued about the proper balance between local flexibility and federal control. On one end of the continuum stood the Nixon administration, suggesting very limited federal intervention in the affairs of cities and counties. On the other end of the continuum was the Senate's determination to maintain high levels of federal involvement. Senator Robert Taft (R.-Ohio) strongly stated the underlying concern of many senators:

> The essence of any community development program—housing and physical development and redevelopment—probably deals more fundamentally with the problems of economic and racial integration, which have proved so difficult for localities to tackle even with strong federal directives, than any other federal program. Because of such problems, I feel that community development is one of the least suitable types of program areas for a totally "hands-off" revenue sharing approach.[25]

The compromise language agreed on in the Congress outlined various statements of national purpose and demands for assurances from participating cities and counties. Yet, as the Advisory Commission on Intergovernmental Relations noted, "The contradictions inherent in the compromise cannot be overlooked. . . . What emerges, then, as the real test is how these 'conditions' are applied in actual administrative practice."[26] The legislation handed broad authority to local elected officials, but their precise responsibility to the federal government for the way they chose to use CDBG funds was not clearly defined.

The Community Development Act's citizen participation objectives were a legacy of the War on Poverty programs of the 1960s in general, and more specifically an outgrowth of the Model Cities program and the urban renewal program's attempt to increase citizen participation as early as 1967. But the procedures outlined for citizen participation in the Community Development Block Grant program departed sharply from the extensive community participation ideology of the Model Cities program. CDBG elicits guarantees that communities have given citizens "adequate information" about the program, "held public hearings to obtain the views of citizens," and generally "provided citizens an adequate opportunity to participate in the development of the application" (Section 104 [a]). But the law also makes it clear that local officials are responsible for the final decisions about how CDBG funds will be applied.

CDBG's supporters, such as Representative Garry Brown (R.-Mich.), claimed that the law represented "nothing but hope for greater citizen participation. It will bring the city fathers closer to the citizens than to Washington."[27] But skeptics, critical of a retreat from the community power model of citizen participation, commented, "Performance criteria on the role of poverty area residents . . . are weak and diffuse and suggest a return to the very limited city-wide advisory boards used in conjunction with urban renewal more than a decade ago."[28] Given the vague policy statements in the law, it is not surprising that people with divergent perspectives differently interpreted the potential impact of citizen participation.

Elected Officials

Compared to their participation during the categorical era, elected officials have taken a greater part in community development programs under CDBG. The movement of power toward elected officials and away from the staffs of special purpose agencies, such as Urban Renewal Authorities and Model Cities Administrations, had been encouraged by the HUD Annual Arrangements program. The pace quickened with the passage of CDBG because it did not require the establishment of special purpose units to receive funds as most categorical programs did.

A study carried out by the Brookings Institution in sixty-two communities over a two-year period documents the increasing involvement of elected officials and their dominance of both procedural and substantive aspects of CDBG policymaking and administration.[29] Their report on the second year of the program indicates that political executives and their staffs continued to be the most influential decision-makers, but that citizen groups and city and county legislators became more important.[30]

Though elected officials, particularly those in larger jurisdictions, delegated authority for drafting community development plans to their staffs,[31] elected officials became deeply involved in distributing community development projects to specific neighborhoods within cities or counties.[32] Mayors, city council members, and county executives participated most actively in politically sensitive decisions about who would benefit from CDBG programs.[33]

Citizen Participation

The involvement of citizens as individuals and groups in community development decisions varied substantially among communities, but most observers agreed that the statutory requirements for hearings and public notification were met.[34] Illustrative of the range of approaches to citizen participation are the findings of the Brookings study of sixty-one communities: thirteen held only public city-wide hearings; seventeen had general and neighborhood hearings; eighteen appointed a citizen advisory committee; and thirteen held hearings to supplement the advisory committee's work.[35]

Evidence assessing the influence of citizen participation on CDBG decision-making also reveals mixed outcomes. A survey of 880 city and county officials, conducted by HUD, found that they viewed citizen participation as the most influential factor shaping "the direction and development of their community development application."[36] In the first year of CDBG, the Brookings field staff rated citizen participation influential in eighteen of the sixty-two communities in their study, influential to a limited extent in twenty-six more, and not at all influential in eighteen communities.[37]

HUD's surveys of citizen participation also demonstrate that citizens were not equally influential in all stages of CDBG planning and administration. They found citizens' impact highest at the planning stages when needs are analyzed and priorities set, lower in the selection of activities for funding and the designation of neighborhoods where projects will be located, and lowest in evaluating program performance.[38]

According to most analysts, the character of citizen participation under the Community Development Act diverged significantly from that under Model Cities, a fact that prompted criticism from such interest groups as the National Urban League, the National Association for the Advancement of Colored People, and the Southern Regional Council.[39] The power of citizen organizations established during the Model Cities era declined, their role often taken over by city-wide groups. People who participated in CDBG program decisions also differed from those who belonged to the Model Cities organizations. Citizen participation became more broad based under CDBG: there was less domination by low-income and white neighborhoods.[40] Competition for a finite resource, the CDBG allocation, became more intense.

The Federal Role

A congressional staff review of HUD's performance under the community development law observed, "An issue here is how can HUD satisfy its administrative responsibilities and at the same time meet the mandate for decentralized decision making."[41] The record suggests that HUD had difficulty walking the tightrope between the dual requirements. Throughout CDBG's history the department has been both passive observer and aggressive federal overseer.

During the first year of the program, HUD followed Assistant Secretary for Community Development David Meeker's admonition: "No second guessing of local officials and a minimum of red tape."[42] HUD denied funding to three out of 1,324 cities and counties in the first year and to eight in the second, because they had refused to revise their Housing Assistance Plans to meet more realistic goals for low-income housing.[43] HUD further demonstrated its preference for a low profile by not publishing a handbook outlining appropriate community development strategies, by refusing requests to bolster citizen participation guidelines, and by leaving undefined the meaning of the law's "maximum feasible priority" clause relating to low- and moderate-income groups.[44] Some local officials lambasted HUD for "leaving too much discretion at the outset . . . and then later ruling certain activities ineligible" in subsequent program audits.[45]

Within a year members of Congress and interest groups were assailing HUD's reluctance to enforce the national goals that they deemed important. In the second and third years of the act a stronger HUD role emerged, leading local officials to complain that HUD was "recategorizing" community development programs.[46] HUD's increased intervention in local decisions was stimulated, in part, by a federal court ruling that it had violated the law by approving grants to towns that had not adequately assessed "the housing needs of low and moderate income persons" under the HAP section of the law.[47] Though this case was later overturned in an appeal by the affected communities,[48] HUD's immediate response was to issue more detailed guidelines and to make more thorough reviews of local plans and performance reports.[49]

The general trend toward stronger federal oversight sharply increased in early 1977 after the turnover in national administation and the appointment of Secretary Harris to HUD. Testifying before the Senate Banking, Housing, and Urban Affairs Committee, she characteized HUD's condition upon her arrival:

> I discovered . . . an absence of the essential degree of energy, direction, and will required to carry out the mandates of the Congress in the areas of housing and community development. The community development block grant program was being administered in a way which permitted localities to expend grant funds without adequate regard for the interests of their low- and moderate-income residents.[50]

She reiterated the department's commitment to enforcing the national goals of the CDBG program. Perhaps the best measure of its new posture, however, was HUD's new definition of the term "maximum feasible priority" as expenditure of at least 75 percent of a community's grant on low- and moderate-income groups—a policy that was eventually struck down by Congress.

Explaining Who Governs: The Model Applied

Elected officials are more involved in CDBG programs than they were during the categorical era, but they continue to delegate all but the more politically sensitive issues, such as who will benefit from CDBG funds, to their staffs. Methods of citizen participation and its influence varied, but the scope of participants widened. The federal role began on a low-key level but escalated and became more aggressive during the years of the program.

Policy Standards and Resources. CDBG and its revisions left federal and local implementors with substantial freedom to define their roles and responsibilities. Consequently, the statute itself was not a highly influential factor in determining governance patterns. The statute did help to structure the decision-making process, however.

1. The act subjugates special purpose authorities to general purpose government officials. Elected officials had few opportunities to shape community development strategies before CDBG; the new law allowed them to participate fully in making program choices.[51]

2. The statute required less citizen participation under CDBG than under the Model Cities program. Model Cities mandated organizational structures; citizen involvement in planning, policymaking, and administration; election of representatives by neighborhood residents; and financial compensation for citizen participants. CDBG's broad directions in the 1974 version of the law imply that citizen involvement can be restricted to the planning stage. Model Cities gave power to the low-income residents of target areas; CDBG lodges power with elected officials and encourages a community-wide approach to citizen participation.[52]

3. The policy permits flexible and shifting responses by the federal bureaucracy. Substantially different approaches to carrying out federal responsibilities emerged between 1975 and 1978, despite the basic stability of statutory provisions. The contradictory national goals contained in CDBG also help explain HUD's changing postures. For instance, the law instructs communities to target their programs to low- and moderate-income areas, but it also promotes programs that will enhance the dispersion of low-income groups. Consequently, because it was virtually impossible for HUD to enforce all the objectives of the act simultaneously, the department frequently focused on procedural objectives.[53]

The National Policy Environment. The national policy environment, including congressional and interest group pressures, was important in explaining HUD's role in CDBG and influencing citizen participation.

The history of HUD's involvement in CDBG confirms the observation that program implementation is "a continuation into another arena of the political process.''[54] HUD was constantly pressured by external groups demanding *more* or *less* federal intervention. Civil rights groups pursued civil suits to force a more assertive HUD role. Public interest groups such as the National League of Cities, representing the concerns of local government, argued for a less intrusive HUD.[55]

Key members of the Senate and House of Representatives insisted that HUD implement CDBG in accord with the philosophies they expressed during its legislative development. The Senate wanted more oversight by HUD, the House, less. In 1976 at CDBG's first major oversight hearings Senator William Proxmire, chairman of the Senate committee responsible for community development programs, criticized Assistant Secretary Meeker for failing to exercise HUD's power:

> What isn't clear is whether the program that you have been administering is the program Congress passed. . . . We have earlier in these hearings received a catalog of HUD's sins and omissions. Some critics say HUD has been implementing until relatively recently the administration's [urban special] revenue sharing bill.[56]

When a stronger HUD emerged during the Carter administration, one senior member of the House Subcommittee on Housing and Community Development accused Secretary Harris of administering law "contrary to the clear intent of Congress."[57] Congress's revision of the law in 1978 made its intent clearer: HUD should not try to dictate local priorities.

Initially HUD preferred that communities develop their own approaches to citizen participation—a position upheld in several court challenges.[58] But in the subsequent years of CDBG, HUD exerted more influence by insisting upon evidence of adequate citizen participation in reviews of applications and in performance evaluations.[59] Overall, HUD's oversight seemed to enhance citizen participation where the agency chose to raise the issue.[60]

The Local Policy Environment. Several aspects of the local policy environment help explain the roles of elected officials, citizens, and the federal government.

1. Elected officials' participation in CDBG programs increased because demands from groups within their jurisidctions often drew them into the process. Legislators increased their attention to CDBG, responding to constituent demands by holding legislative forums where citizen groups could air their concerns.[61] Mayors and county elected officials were thrust into CDBG politics in order to deal with conflicts arising over which areas of the community would get community development projects and services and to mediate disputes between special purpose government agencies.[62] The new politics of community development often demanded personal involvement by elected officials.

2. The nature and scope of citizen participation were primarily shaped by the attitudes of local officials toward citizen involvement. Brookings researchers report that, in 80 percent of the communities in their sample, elected officials took the citizen participation requirement "seriously."[63] But their motivations for encouraging citizen participation and the extent to which citizens were actually allowed to have input varied. For example, some officials delegated controversial CDBG decisions to citizen advisory groups in order to escape full responsibility for tough choices.[64] Whatever the approach chosen, however, the elected officials' attitudes were paramount because the statute permitted local elected officials to structure the citizen advisory committees and otherwise to mold the process of gathering citizen opinions.[65]

The other critical feature of the local policy environment that shaped citizen participation was the nature of group demands. Generally, communities with a history of high citizen activity under the Model Cities or other federal programs had higher citizen involvement in CDBG than those without such experience, according to the Brookings analysis.[66] The city-wide emphasis of CDBG also brought into the political process lower middle class whites and other neighborhood groups who demanded more influence over community development decisions.

3. The extent of *HUD's influence* in each community was also determined by the attitudes of the local staff and elected officials. HUD's influence was greatest on procedural issues, where elected officials were less concerned with the outcomes.[67] HUD also prevailed more often in smaller communities and counties that lacked experience in dealing with HUD. Larger communities more often resisted its attempts to guide their programs.[68]

Summary

Patterns of CDBG governance are determined principally by the local policy environment, especially the attitudes of local officials and the nature of local politics. The national policy environment had only a limited impact on local decision-making, but the federal government's changing involvement in CDBG programs is explained by heated debates at the national level over HUD's role and changes in senior personnel at HUD. Policy standards were the least important factors in the explanation of who governs CDBG because they offered limited guidance to federal and local implementors.

What Is the Impact of Decategorization?
Program Design and Expenditures

CDBG consolidated several diverse categorical programs that had been authorized over a twenty-five-year period. Decategorization or combining programs in a single block grant was supposed to enhance the flexibility of local officials to determine needs and community development strategies. But the Congress denied them total flexibility by interposing several national goals for the use of CDBG funds.

First, CDBG activities had to either benefit low- or moderate-income families, aid in the prevention or elimination of slums and blight, or, if approved by HUD, meet urgent community needs. Second, Congress further elaborated CDBG's purpose by listing seven (and, in the 1977 revision, eight) national objectives. Third, the law enumerated thirteen "eligible activities," such as the completion of urban renewal projects and the improvement of housing conditions through code enforcement.

By authorizing a series of community development activities and providing an indication of acceptable and unacceptable approaches, the law reversed the Model Cities emphasis on social services and gave prominence to physical development or "hardware" projects. Despite all the rhetoric of reform, however, "these substantive objectives [of the law] are still quite general and flexible," according to the staff of a congressional committee charged with CDBG's oversight.[69] Empirical evidence on the types of programs funded and the general approach to community development employed by cities and counties under CDBG is compared below to trends that existed during the categorical era.

Community Development Strategies and
Program Expenditures

Data presented in table 4-2 demonstrate that communities have sharply shifted emphasis away from such programs as urban renewal, Model Cities, and water and sewer construction toward smaller-scale neighborhood improvements and loans for homeowners wishing to rehabilitate their property. When these data are compared with information on CDBG-funded activities grouped differently in table 4-3, the emerging trends in community development programs under the new statute become clearer. Large-scale, long-term urban renewal, such as land clearance through demolition of deteriorating buildings, declined, and smaller, short-term, public works and housing rehabilitation projects increased substantially. HUD's analysis of CDBG programs presents clear evidence that rehabilitation was emphasized. In the first year of the Community Development Act, cities and counties spent $1.00 on rehabilitation loans and grants for every 90 cents they used to acquire property for demolition; from 1966 to 1970, they spent $1.00 on rehabilitation for every $13.00 spent on demolition.[70] Although urban renewal received less attention under CDBG, communities still spent nearly one-fifth of their funds on continuing or closing out projects begun during the categorical period.[71]

Table 4-2

CDBG Program Expenditures for Fiscal Years 1975-1977, Compared to Equivalent Categorical Program Expenditures for Fiscal Years 1968-1972, by Type of Activity

(in percent)

Categorical Program Activity	Categorical Funds 1968 to 1972[a]	CDBS Funds in Similar Categories 1975 to 1977[a]
Urban renewal/neighborhood development[b]	62	30
Housing code enforcement	_[c]	2
Water and sewer[d]	10	2
Neighborhood facilities	2	3
Open space	5	5
Rehabilitation loans	2	10
Model Cities[e]	21	6
Supportive public services[f]	−	9
Neighborhood improvement[f]	−	33
Totals	102[g]	100

Source: U.S., Department of Housing and Urban Development, *Community Development Block Grant, Third Annual Report* (Washington, D.C.: Government Printing Office, 1978), table 18.1, p. 268, and Appendix G, pp. 444-445.

[a]These data exclude deferred, administrative, planning, studies, and contingency amounts.

[b]The CDBG amounts are all funds in UR/NDP areas spent on demolition, historic preservation, public works, relocation, and so on.

[c]Less than 1 percent was budgeted for this category.

[d]All water and sewer expenditures not in UR and NDP areas.

[e]The CDBG amounts are all funds in Model Neighborhood Areas spent on acquisition for redevelopment, relocation, demolition, housing, public services, and so on.

[f]These programs were not funded under the categorical programs.

[g]Total sums to more than 100 percent due to rounding.

According to HUD's analysis, communities spent more CDBG money on public facilities improvements and housing rehabilitation and less for demolition, land clearance, and social services than they had before. Approximately 60 percent of the program funds in fiscal years 1975 through 1977 were spent on the elimination of slums and blight and rehabilitation and conservation of the housing stock. In contrast, less than 1 percent was directed at historic preservation and the reduction of income group isolation.[72] Exceptions to these general patterns occurred in many communities, most significantly urban counties, where much higher proportions of funds were used on community services than on the elimination of slums and blight.[73]

The Brookings Institution used a different method of categorizing community development activities than that used by HUD. Also, the Brookings

Table 4-3

Activities Funded by CDBG Recipients for Fiscal Years 1975-1977
(in percent)

	1975	1976	1977
Redevelopment-related activities[a]	36	28	22
Public works[b]	16	23	29
Housing rehabilitation[c]	15	20	20
Public services	13	11	11
Open space and neighborhood'facilities	6	8	8
Service-related facilities[d]	7	6	6
Water and sewer projects	6	4	3
Code enforcement	2	2	2
Totals[e]	101	102	101

Source: U.S., Department of Housing and Urban Development, *Community Development Block Grants, Third Annual Report* (Washington, D.C.: Government Printing Office, 1978), table 14.1, p. 241.

[a]Includes such activities as land acquisition, completion of urban renewal projects, and relocation costs.

[b]Public works projects other than water and sewer projects, such as street improvements.

[c]Majority of the funds go to loans and grants for residents or others to improve existing housing.

[d]These funds typically are used to build or maintain recreational facilities or programs for the elderly.

[e]Totals sum to more than 100 percent due to rounding.

sample, unlike HUD's, is not a random, stratified sample representative of all grant recipients. Nevertheless, data from their study provide useful comparisons with the HUD information even though the information is not equivalent. The Brookings study found that only 11 percent of all CDBG funds were spent on social services and facilities such as health, education, and child care. In contrast, cities and counties in their sample spent 34 percent of their CDBG grants on housing and neighborhood conservation projects. Thirty-one percent of the funds provide police and security services, planning and general development, such as the construction of parks, sidewalks, and streets.[74]

*Explaining Community Development Strategies:
The Model Applied*

The two-year study of community development programs by the Brookings Institution succinctly summarizes the major changes in community development strategies documented above: "Communities are shifting to smaller-scale, more diversified programs. Work on large-scale urban renewal projects . . . is being stretched out or completed. . . . Housing rehabilitation has become an important community development activity under CDBG. . . . Social services, the primary focus of the model cities program, have declined sharply as an activity under CDBG. . . .[75]

Policy Standards and Resources. CDBG's list of thirteen "eligible activities" encouraged communities to concentrate on physical redevelopment projects and strongly discouraged expenditures on social service programs. Eight of the thirteen community development approaches legitimized by the statute involve physical development projects. And social service programs may only be funded if they are supportive of physical redevelopment projects. Despite these features of the law that directed local communities to emphasize national goals, the overall statute provided ample flexibility. For example, the increased freedom afforded local government officials over the design of community development projects encouraged them to develop smaller-scale projects such as neighborhood housing rehabilitation.[76]

CDBG's resources were inadequate to permit new large-scale projects. Though funding for community development programs in fiscal year 1975 represented a 15 percent increase over money available during the categorical era, the small increase was dispersed among 40 percent more communities.[77] In addition, the law mandated the completion of ongoing urban renewal projects, practically forcing many communities to spend large sums of their block grants on these projects.[78] The lack of additional resources in many communities, as well as the restrictions on how CDBG funds could be applied, increased the likelihood that funds left over after commitments to urban renewal projects were met would fund small-scale, short-term projects.

At the general level, the policy's standards helped shape local community development strategies, but there is substantial evidence indicating that the law's provisions were not of overriding importance. Under the law's general statement of national goals, local officials retained broad authority to design specific projects. Thus, according to one study, local officials typically placed locally designed projects into the national program categories for reporting to HUD after they had made their selections.[79] Moreover, the range of eligible activities authorized by law is so extensive that virtually any community development activity could be funded and justified.

The National Policy Environment. The federal government's impact on the design of local community development strategies was less important than the local policy environment, in part because HUD's field staff had difficulty interpreting which activities were eligible to be funded under the law.[80] Since HUD's staff experienced internal disagreement about the value and appropriateness of some community development programs, it was unable to systematically influence local choices.

Nevertheless, HUD officials helped preserve the status quo by pressing cities and counties to complete their urban renewal projects.[81] Moreover, HUD may have fostered a decline in spending on social service programs by enforcing the *unadopted* 20 percent ceiling on such expenditures. The department frequently forced communities to modify their CDBG applications for failure to adhere to the 20 percent limit on expenditures for social services.[82]

The Local Policy Environment. Several aspects of the local policy environment are significant in accounting for the nature of community development programs under CDBG.

1. The *attitudes of local officials*, their preferences and prejudices about community development programs, had significant effects. Overall, elected officials and their staffs preferred visible physical development projects that could be implemented quickly and with relative ease. Such projects were also favored because they created no built-in obligations to groups who would return year after year and demand continued funding.[83] Aside from their specific preferences, widespread cynicism about the stability of CDBG funding helped explain the heavy reliance on short-term, small-scale projects.[84] Elected officials wanted to have something to show for their involvement in the community development program even if Congress terminated funding after three years.

2. The nature of local program strategies was also shaped by the *characteristics of the local implementing agency*. Communities in which Model Cities programs had existed before CDBG spent larger sums of money on social service programs, in part because professional staffs from the Model Cities agency exerted pressure for continued funding.[85] According to HUD's analysis, social service spending was seven times higher in communities with Model Cities experience than in those without.[86] The exception to the general pattern would be the over seventy urban counties that had very few Model Cities programs but funneled very high proportions of their CDBG funds into social services.

3. Increases in spending for housing rehabilitation and conservation and for public facilities improvements were influenced by *local political considerations*. CDBG brought more participants into the process of allocating community development funds, thus producing demands for wider distribution of those funds. The interplay of local political forces stimulated increases in projects such as fixing streetlights or making curb repairs which can be rapidly mounted in many locations. Over time, such projects contributed to declines in downtown-oriented, large-scale, urban renewal projects promoted by the federal government in the 1960s and early

1970s. Citizen participation, with increased involvement by neighborhood groups and organizations, also reinforced the trend toward neighborhood rehabilitation and other community development projects located in a community's residential areas rather than its business district.[87]

4. Finally, *economic and social conditions* of the communities influenced strategies of community development programming. Cities and counties experiencing the most severe problems of poverty and deterioration of their housing units spread money around the community to address diverse and widespread needs. Communities with less severe problems usually concentrated spending in a limited number of trouble spots and on fewer community development programs.[88]

Summary

Important modifications in community development strategies under the block grant program are explained by the policy standards' emphasis on physical development projects and deemphasis on social services. Though less important, the national policy environment reinforced these general trends. The most important component of the explanation lies in the local policy environment. The attitudes of local elected officials and their response to the politics of community development led to projects designed to capture broad-based political support. Objective measures of community need helped account for overall strategies, but they were not an overriding factor.

Who Benefits from Community Development Block Grants?

Closely related to the community development strategies that emerged under CDBG are the areas of the community and the types of people who benefit from them. Ample evidence has already been provided to demonstrate that the question of how to target community development funds was one of the most controversial issues in the law's development. Although the statute that resulted from the debate did not reserve a proportion of funds for lower income families, it does contain language indicating Congress's concern for these groups.

Congressional intent was contained in three key passages of the law: Section 101 (c) indicated that CDBG's benefits were intended "principally for persons of low and moderate income"; the law's list of national objectives made frequent references to serving low- and moderate-income people; and Section 104 (b) demanded that all grant recipients develop plans that "give maximum feasible priority to activities which will benefit low- or moderate-income families or aid in the prevention of slums and blight." The statements of intent and the certification requirement reflected Congress's general concern that local elected officials would ignore the needs of low-income areas unless they were strongly encouraged to address them.[89]

The Carter administration and Secretary Harris of HUD were not satisfied with the mere espousal of national goals favoring low- and moderate-income groups. But despite the secretary's effort to define "maximum feasible priority" more clearly, the majority of congressmen continued to prefer ambiguous language. The empirical questions addressed here are what share of the resources did low- and moderate-income groups receive from CDBG, and how does this compare with their share of categorical program funds? The analysis describes the direct benefits to low- and moderate-income areas when it is possible to isolate them. Naturally community-wide projects aimed at general economic development and revitalization may bring substantial benefits to lower income groups in the long run.

Benefit Distribution under CDBG

Unfortunately, it is not possible to answer directly the question of who benefits from community development programs, because no one has undertaken the enormously difficult and costly task of collecting information on the characteristics of people who participate in various CDBG-funded projects and services. Several alternative approaches for estimating the benefits from CDBG programs are available, however. Table 4-4 presents a summary of the major studies of benefit distribution by HUD, the Brookings Institution, and the National Association of Housing and Rehabilitation Officers (NAHRO). Data reported in Parts I, II, and III of the table relied on the so-called "sociospatial method" that locates census tracts in which CDBG projects are delivered and categorizes those tracts by income and in relation to the median income of the area, based on the 1970 census. The percent of funds that "benefit" different categories of census tracts can then be calculated by aggregating the separate projects.

Though this is the most common method used to answer the question of who benefits, its shortcomings should be noted.[90] First, the law did not define what is meant by "area"; most researchers used the median income of the Standard Metropolitan Statistical Area (SMSA) as the basis for ranking the income level of a given census tract. A few others, such as NAHRO, used the city's median income. The area with which one compares CDBG-funded census tracts will increase or decrease the number of tracts that are defined as low- or moderate-income. Second, the determination of what

Table 4-4

CDBG Funds Distributed to Low- and Moderate-Income Areas, as Reported by Various Studies
(in percent)

	1975	1976	1977
I. When the SMSA median income is compared with the median incomes in the census tracts.			
Estimates reported by	*1975*	*1976*	*1977*
Department of Housing and Urban Development (HUD)	69	62	62
The Brookings Institution	52	N.A.	N.A.
II. When the city's median income is compared with the median incomes of the census tracts.			
Estimates reported by	*1975*	*1976*	
HUD	N.A.	48	
NAHRO	51	44	
III. When the data are standardized to assume that administrative costs provide no income area specific benefits.			
Estimates reported by	*1975*	*1976*	
HUD	47	46	
The Brookings Institution	56	N.A.	
NAHRO	49	46	
IV. When CDBG projects are assigned to the low- and moderate-income category if (1) the project has a low- and moderate-income eligibility requirement, or (2) the project is delivered in a census tract composed of a majority of low- and moderate-income people.			
Estimate reported by	*1975*	*1976*	*1977*
HUD	64	62	62

Sources: HUD data are from U.S., Department of Housing and Urban Development, *Community Development Block Grants: Third Annual Report* (Washington, D.C.: Government Printing Office, March 1978), pp. 55, 56. Brookings data are from Richard P. Nathan et al., *Block Grants for Community Development* (Washington, D.C.: Government Printing Office), table 8-1, p. 308. NAHRO data are from NAHRO *Newsletter* XI:1 (January 3, 1977).

levels constitute low and moderate income is also somewhat arbitrary. Studies reported in table 4-4 defined low-income census tracts as those with incomes at or below 50 percent of the SMSA's median or city income level. Moderate-income areas were defined as those with 51 percent to 80 percent of the median income of the SMSA or city. Other income tracts fell above the 80 percent cutoff point. Third, census tracts are often very heterogeneous because they can encompass a large area and contain average populations of around 4,000. Consequently, assigning benefits by geographic area may overestimate or underestimate the benefits to various income groups if only a small proportion of the tract's population actually gains from it. Finally, some projects, such as housing rehabilitation, may be designed to eventually benefit nonresidents with income levels that differ from income levels in the census tract's population. Thus the analysis of short-term benefits obscures the long-run impact of the projects.

Using the methods described above in an analysis of nearly 150 communities, HUD found that services to low- and moderate-income areas declined from 69 to 62 percent from fiscal year 1975 to fiscal year 1977. Also, as reported in Part I of table 4-4, the Brookings Institution estimated low- and moderate-income benefits at 52 percent. Because the Brookings sample is not statistically representative of all communities in the United States, as the HUD sample is, its results are not equivalent.

Part II of table 4-4 displays estimates of low- and moderate-income benefits when the census tracts where CDBG activities are funded are compared with the city's median income. As would be expected, this basis of comparison causes the estimates to drop significantly. For example, in fiscal year 1976, the HUD estimate drops from 62 percent under the SMSA comparison to 48 percent using the city median income comparison. NAHRO's data also indicate in the second year of the program a decrease of 7 percent in the amount of CDBG funds going to low- and moderate-income census tracts.

Estimates of low- and moderate-income benefits are again altered when the assumptions reported in Part III of table 4-4 are applied. Data reported in Parts I and II of the table were calculated by assuming that low- and moderate-income families would receive the identical proportion of benefits from funds spent on administration and city-wide activities as they would from projects delivered in the census tracts. In Part III the opposite assumption is made, namely that city-wide projects and administrative costs do not benefit low- and moderate-income areas at all. When this adjustment is applied to HUD's data, for example, estimates of fiscal year 1976 benefits are reduced from 62 percent to 46 percent.

A somewhat different method for calculating low- and moderate-income benefits is reported in Part IV of table 4-4.[91] Using data from their sample of nearly 150 communities, HUD assigned benefits to the low- and moderate-income category if the CDBG project had income eligibility requirements restricting benefits to low- and moderate-income people. When the project didn't have such restrictions, it could only be assigned to the low- and moderate-income category if the project took place in a census tract that was composed of a majority of low- and moderate-income families. This method avoids some of the problems associated with the sociospatial approach reported in Parts I, II, and III of the table, but it still suffers from imprecision in assigning benefits and the reliance on self-reporting by communities. Nevertheless, of the methods reported, these data are the most representative of the national experience under CDBG and probably the most reliable estimates of low- and moderate-income benefits. They show that low- and moderate-income benefits represent about three-fifths of the program funds during fiscal years 1975 to 1977, with only a slight drop of about 2 percent during the period.

Data from the studies of benefit distribution also suggest that benefits to the lowest income areas were limited. Employing the city median income method, NAHRO's study of eighty-six communities pegged benefits to low-income census tracts at 12 percent in 1975 and 10 percent in 1976.[92] HUD's analysis of 147 communities fixed the low-income figure at only 7 percent. Brookings researchers found considerably higher percentages going to low-income census tracts, using the SMSA median income as the basis of comparison. In their study of fifty-two communities in the first year of CDBG, they estimated that 29 percent of all funds went to low-income areas—those at 50 percent or less of the SMSA's median income.[93] Given the methodological shortcomings noted above, distinctions between benefits going to low-income versus moderate-income areas must be judged as suggestive at best.

Data from the Brookings study also indicate substantial variation in the distribution of benefits in divergent types of communities. Funds expended in low- and moderate-income census tracts comprised, on the average, 60 percent of all funds in the central cities in their sample, 53 percent in nonmetropolitan areas, and only 20 percent in smaller outlying cities.[94] Moreover, the Brookings analysts estimated benefits to low- and moderate-income families to be as high as 100 percent in some communities and zero percent in others.[95] HUD's data on urban counties in fiscal year 1975 also reveal the differences among grant recipients. While metropolitan cities in their sample planned to put 71 percent of their CDBG funds into low- and moderate-income tracts, urban counties planned only 37 percent in similar areas.[96]

Whether one uses the HUD, NAHRO, or Brookings data, it is clear that *low-income* census tracts received a small proportion of CDBG funds. More clearly, the data show that *low and moderate-income* areas combined received between half and three-fifths of the total allocations from fiscal year 1975 to fiscal year 1977. Unfortunately, there is no reliable data on categorical grant money spent in these areas, but several useful comparisons help illustrate the differences between CDBG and the categorical programs.

One sign of the change in benefits during the CDBG era was the drop in the proportion of funds spent in areas that benefited under the categorical programs. HUD's analysis, for example, found that CDBG funds allocated for areas serviced by categorical programs declined from 58 percent in fiscal year 1975 to 49 percent in fiscal year 1977, with the major decline in former urban renewal areas.[97] Another study comparing program funding in five

California Model Cities neighborhoods, conducted by Rufus Browning, Dale Marshall, and David Tabb, shows an average decrease of 21 percent in CDBG funds going to Model neighborhood areas. This occurred despite the fact that the total amount of money flowing into the city as a whole remained constant. According to these analysts: "Once the cities were not forced by federal requirements to target grant money to the areas that they had identified as most needy, they spread the money to other areas. . . ."[98]

Evidence on the exact extent of change between the categorical and CDBG periods is less precise than one would like, but the general tendency of CDBG recipients to spread programs to wider clientele groups in their communities is supported. CDBG has tripled the number of census tracts that benefited from community development funds during the categorical era. Only 38 percent of those new census tracts meet the definition of low- and moderate-income used above. In contrast, "80 percent of the census tracts receiving assistance prior to 1974 were low- and moderate-income," according to HUD's estimates.[99]

The spreading effect and this shift in the types of census tracts served by CDBG programs demonstrate the close linkage between community development strategies and patterns of benefit distribution. Many communities have followed a triage approach to community development. "Triage" is a battlefield term for dividing the wounded into three groups—those who can be saved only with immediate medical attention, those who cannot be saved, and those who will pull through without assistance. Applied to strategies of community development by urban economist Anthony Downs and others, it refers to a strategy of concentrating funds in so-called transitional neighborhoods. Transitional areas are those which face imminent decline and blight unless actions to retard the decay are taken.

Various studies of CDBG document the prevalence of the triage strategy. HUD's analysis of over 140 communities in 1977 reported that almost half of the funds were budgeted to neighborhoods that were classified as being in "early-to-moderate" decline, while one-third of CDBG funds went to the "worst" areas of the communities.[100] Similar conclusions were reached by other analysts, such as Victor Bach of the LBJ School, who commented on the school's six-city study which found that CDBG funds were "more likely to be [spent in] the marginally deteriorated, more conservable, moderate-income neighborhoods of the city than the most blighted and impoverished areas."[101]

Explaining Who Benefits: The Model Applied

The switch from categorical programs to CDBG brought about moderate change in the distribution of benefits from community development programs. Though there are no reliable data on how funds were distributed during the categorical period, the general trend under CDBG is to spread the funds to a greater number of areas in communities. During the years of the CDBG programs, there has been a slight decline in program resources for low- and moderate-income groups. Overall lower-income areas receive between a half and three-fifths of the CDBG benefits. Variations among cities and counties are substantial, however.

Policy Standards and Resources. Three features of the statute help explain who benefits from community development programs.

1. A larger and somewhat different set of communities received funds under the CDBG program than had participated during the categorical era. CDBG's 1974 formula favored newer, growing cities and suburbs. According to the Brookings Institution, funding to central cities increased 1.3 percent over comparable allocations from the categorical programs, whereas resources for urban counties increased by 78 percent in the first year.[102] Moreover, the central cities' proportion of total CDBG funds declined substantially. Thus the flow of funds set in motion by the law increased the number of communities participating in community development activities. Because those communities had different population characteristics than did the categorical program communities, changes in benefit distribution outcomes were inevitable. Also, the reduced size of the CDBG grant in some communities hindered efforts to address major problems in the worst areas. Lacking sufficient resources to attack the most troubled sections of their cities and bring about significant improvement, local officials often put their CDBG funds into neighborhoods where more limited funds could have a noticeable impact.

Had the 1974 formula continued and the hold-harmless provision been eliminated, the loss of funds for central cities with large low-income and minority populations would have been substantial. But the 1977 dual formulas halted the decline in funds for those cities and may contribute to stabilizing national patterns of benefits to low-income and minority groups.

2. The law was ambiguous about who should benefit from community development programs, and its revisions preserved that ambiguity. It identified at least two primary objectives—low- or moderate-income groups *or* the prevention of slums and blight. The juxtaposition of these two objectives caused considerable confusion among federal and local program administrators. According to a congressional staff report, "Because blight is a relative term, activities directed toward its prevention and elimination have not necessarily directly benefited low- and moderate-income persons."[103] The 1977 revisions of CDBG seemed to given symbolic emphasis to lower income areas by modifying the law to stress low- *and* moderate-income people instead of low- *or* moderate-income people. But a provision permitting

communities to establish programs "to induce higher income people to remain in, or return to, the community," was also inserted.[104]

3. Finally, CDBG had multiple conflicting purposes, which invited widely different interpretations of congressional intent. Rhetorically, emphasis was placed on serving the needs of low-income people and on concentrating community development resources in the nation's most blighted areas. But there was also much emphasis on preventing blighting conditions and expanding housing opportunities for low-income groups beyond the boundaries of the urban inner city.[105] In short, the law laid out contradictory strategies for community development, and, therefore, rather than resolving differences of opinion, it kindled debate among actors in the political system.

The National Policy Environment. The impact on benefit distribution of HUD and other national actors was as important as the broad impact of the legislation, but probably not as significant as the local policy environment. Initially, HUD avoided defining key clauses in the law that related to who benefits—a policy for which they were widely criticized.[106] Citing evidence to suggest that high-income people were getting more aid from CDBG than low-income people, Senator William Proxmire lectured Assistant Secretary David Meeker at CDBG oversight hearings in 1976.

> You are helping moderate and middle [income people] maybe, but the people who don't get the assistance are the ones who, of course, usually under too many circumstances don't get it. . . . These are the people who don't vote. They don't have any economic clout. . . . They can be neglected both by a Congress and city council with impunity. . . . This is why we tried to put into law, provisions that would work to their benefit because we think they are the ones who need the assistance.

Assistant Secretary Meeker responded:

> You also put into law, Mr. Chairman, some elements which allow this situation to be the way it is. You said that the continuation of urban renewal activities was an eligible expense. A substantial amount of the money that you are identifying there in high income neighborhoods is in fact continuation and completion of urban renewal activities which are largely down-town oriented . . . [and which do not have an] appreciable amount of low-income people.[107]

Even during the initial years of CDBG's implementation, when HUD chose to raise the issue, it favored higher benefits for low-income people and often succeeded in increasing them, according to most analysts.[108] In addition, HUD's narrow definition of the "urgent needs" clause in the law that could have permitted communities to avoid the low- and moderate-income provisions altogether helped foster higher proportions of funds for the poor.[109] But HUD's policy of prohibiting construction and housing aid in severely impoverished neighborhoods with high minority populations prevented projects from being launched in the worst areas of some cities. Designed to promote racial and economic integration, this policy frequently lowered the amount of aid going to the most blighted neighborhoods.[110]

The turnover in HUD's leadership brought about by the election of Jimmy Carter had a major influence on HUD policy toward benefit distribution. Secretary Harris issued tighter regulations governing the "maximum feasible priority" clause, ordered reviews of local programs that resulted in reprogramming of funds,[111] and chided local officials to "direct development and housing programs toward the benefit of low and moderate income citizens."[112] Linking compliance with the Housing Assistance Plan's goals for low-income housing to the block grants, Secretary Harris threatened grant termination for cities and counties that failed to accept low-cost housing for the poor.[113]

The department's position pleased some senators and representatives and interest groups, but it angered local officials, whose Washington-based representatives attacked HUD's stance, and it did not please a majority of Congress.[114] According to the *Congressional Quarterly*, the 1978 CDBG reauthorization restricting HUD's intervention in local priorities "represented a defeat for HUD Secretary Harris, who sought to use the threat of rejecting community development grants (and the loss of money) to prod communities into channeling more money to projects that, in HUD's view, had an immediate benefit for low and moderate income families and neighborhoods."[115]

The Local Policy Environment. Several aspects of the local policy environment explain who benefits from CDBG.

1. The *economic and social conditions* of the community affected the nature of community development strategies and benefit distribution, but shared influence with other factors. HUD visited eighteen communities in 1977 in order to examine their creation of community development plans and concluded that the selection of target areas was usually influenced by some objective criteria of need, such as housing conditions or the income of the area's population. The department noted, however, that other nonobjective factors such as citizen demands and "political pressure" came into play in selecting target areas where CDBG projects would be mounted.[116]

The Brookings Institution's study of benefit distribution also found that communities with higher levels of poverty tended to spend more money in low- and moderate-income areas. But this relationship was only a moderate one.[117] After a second year of observation, Brookings researchers concluded "that the range and severity of community problems is . . . more important than the structure of the decision making process in determining a jurisdiction's *overall approach to commmunity development"* (emphasis added). They also noted, however, that the local political process was important in determining where to spend CDBG funds after those broad strategic choices were made.[118] Further evidence that local economic conditions do not dictate patterns of benefit distribution is added by the research of Browning, Marshall, and Tabb in ten California cities. Specifically, they found a weak relationship between the percentage of minorities in each city's population and the amount of CDBG funds allocated to minority areas within the community.[119]

2. Local program funding decisions affected the distribution of CDBG money to lower-income groups in two senses. First, decisions about general community development strategies have implications for the kinds of areas where projects will be funded. For example, the increasingly popular housing rehabilitation programs were frequently targeted to transitional neighborhoods where fewer low-income residents reside.

Second, communities with experience in Model Cities programs were somewhat more likely to allocate large amounts of money to low- and moderate-income groups, but not always. Previous experience with the Model Cities program apparently had the potential of increasing or decreasing program benefits for the poor. Consider the Brookings study, which found that communities with Model Cities programs during the categorical era "allocated almost 50 percent more benefits to lower-income groups than . . . non-model cities."[120]

In contrast, Browning, Marshall, and Tabb report a decline in benefits to lower-income groups in model cities, explaining that officials were reluctant to continue funding areas of the city that had already received substantial federal aid. Officials could not justify continued or increased support in the face of political demands from areas of the city that had been deprived of community development funds in the past.[121] The central factor that reconciles these divergent observations is the structure of local interest group politics. Communities with highly mobilized and influential model cities groups were able to retain program funds. Weak model cities organizations lost in the struggle with other groups in the community.

3. *Local politics* and the *attitudes of political officials* contribute importantly to explanations of CDBG program benefits. Indeed, most major studies of CDBG decision-making agree that local elected officials "tended to choose the broadest interpretation" of the law's low- and moderate-income objectives.[122] While some local officials held strong preferences for serving the poor with community development programs,[123] most of them favored spreading the CDBG funds across many areas of their communities. The principal explanation for their actions stemmed from the "political dynamics" of CDBG, which Victor Bach of the LBJ School of Public Affairs summarized:

> Competing demands of numerous subareas and neighborhoods for a piece of the community development pie make the program politically sensitive. Neighborhood-based organizations and associations, carrying large numbers of voting constituents behind them, are emerging with some force on the program either through informal channels of influence with elected officials or through subarea representation on elective citizen participatory bodies. . . . As a result mayors and city council members have to be sold on the program in terms of its distributive consequences for key constituencies. High level CD staff are in frequent consultation with the mayor concerning areas targeted for development activity. . . . The political equilibrium which grows out of this process is a form of consensus-building through the dispersion of limited funds among competing subareas.[124]

In short, the most important factors accounting for CDBG decisions about program beneficiaries were the local political coalition and the attitudes of local elected officials toward serving low- and moderate-income groups.

4. Related to the general impact of local politics is the influence of *citizen participation*. The nature of citizen participation in community development block grant programs tended to increase the "spreading effect" and thus reduced benefits for low- and moderate-income groups, according to most observers.[125] The public's impact on *who benefits* depends upon *who participates*. Most analysts found that CDBG's emphasis on citywide participation drew a broader cross section of groups into the decision-making process than did the community power strategy followed under the Model Cities and other War on Poverty programs. The new groups brought into CDBG outnumbered the poor and minorities who used to have the advantage because they faced no competition for funds in many programs. Of course, there were cities where strong organizations representing the poor succeeded in capturing more funds for their constituencies, but these groups usually appeared when local elected officials sympathized with their demands.[126] The general trend was in the opposite direction.

Summary

The analysis provides some insights into how and why community development programs are distributed. Local economic and social conditions are important but seem to play a subordinate role to community development strategies, the attitudes of political officials, and local politics, including the process of citizen participation. The vague and conflicting language of the law, its formula that spreads money to larger numbers of communities, and an initially reserved role on the part of HUD, reinforced benefit distribution to fewer low-income areas. Shifts in HUD's policy probably stimulated increased benefits for the poor, but congressional action to restrain HUD may have reduced the department's attempts to alter the flow of program benefits.

Notes

1. As quoted in U.S., Advisory Commission on Intergovernmental Relations, *Community Development: The Workings of a Federal-Local Block Grant* (Washington, D.C.: Government Printing Office, 1977), p. 10 (hereafter ACIR, *Community Development*).

2. "Cities Win More Say on HUD Grants," *Congressional Quarterly Weekly Report* 36 (1978):3218.

3. ACIR, *Community Development*, pp. 3-4.

4. Ibid., p. 1.

5. Excellent summaries of the legislative history of CDBG may be found in ACIR, *Community Development*; Richard P. Nathan et al., *Block Grants for Community Development* (Washingtron, D.C.: Government Printing Office, 1977); and *Congressional Quarterly Almanac* 30 (1974).

6. U.S. Senator Edmund Muskie (D.-Maine), as quoted in Rochelle L. Stanfield, "Are Brighter Days Ahead for the Nation's Decaying Cities?" *National Journal Reports* 8 (1976):1522.

7. ACIR, *Community Development*, p. 5.

8. As reported in *The Congressional Quarterly Almanac* 27 (1971):63-A.

9. Richard P. Nathan et al., *Block Grants for Community Development* (Washington, D.C.: Government Printing Office, 1977), p. 37 (hereafter Nathan et al., *Block Grants*).

10. ACIR, *Community Development*, p. 8.

11. John L. Moore, "Outlook Improves for Passage of Community Development Bill," *National Journal Reports* 6 (1974):556.

12. Ibid., p. 557.

13. ACIR, *Community Development*, p. 10.

14. For a good summary of the law see Arthur J. Magida, "Major Programs Revised to Stress Community Control," *National Journal Reports* 6 (1974):1369-1379.

15. For a detailed description of the funding formula and how it works see U.S., Department of Housing and Urban Development, *Community Development Block Grant Program: Second Annual Report* (Washington, D.C.: Government Printing Office, 1976), p.. 15 (hereafter HUD, *CDBG—2nd Annual Report*).

16. All citations to the statute refer to Title I of the "Housing and Community Development Act of 1974," Public Law 93-383, and will be made by section number.

17. For a good summary of the 1977 reauthorization see *Congressional Quarterly Almanac* 33 (1977):126-136; and Dommel et al., *Decentralizing Community Development* (Washington, D.C.: Government Printing Office, 1978), pp. 15-21.

18. See, for example, Rochelle L. Stanfield, "Government Seeks the Right Formula for Community Development Funds," *National Journal Reports* 9 (1977):238.

19. For a thorough description of the new formulas and how they work see U.S., Department of Housing and Urban Development, *Community Development Block Grant Program: Directory of Allocations for Fiscal Year 1978* (Washington, D.C.: Government Printing Office, 1978), p. iii.

20. Dommel et al., *Decentralizing Community Development*, p. 21.

21. Rochelle L. Stanfield, "The Latest Community Development Flap—Targeting on the Poor," *National Journal Reports* 9 (1977):1877.

22. As quoted in "House Panel Challenges Harris Move to Boost Grant Aid to Poor," *Congressional Quarterly Weekly Report* 36 (1978):1398.

23. Ibid.

24. "Cities Win More Say on HUD Grants," *Congressional Quarterly Weekly Report* 36 (1978):3218.

25. U.S., Congress, Senate, *The Housing and Community Development Act: Supplemental and Additional Views*, Senate Report 93-593, p. 176.

26. ACIR, *Community Development*, p. 17.

27. Magida, "Major Programs Revised to Stress Community Control," p. 1369.

28. Bernard J. Frieden and Marshall Kaplan, *The Politics of Neglect: Urban Aid from Model Cities to Revenue Sharing* (Cambridge, Mass.: MIT Press, 1975), p. 252.

29. Nathan et al., *Block Grants*, pp. 368, 384; and Dommel et al., *Decentralizing Community Development*, p. 117.

30. Dommel et al., *Decentralizing Community Development*, p. 113.

31. Nathan et al., *Block Grants*, p. 386; and Dommel et al., *Decentralizing Community Development*, p. 121.

32. Nathan et al., *Block Grants*, pp. 387-391.

33. See, for example, U.S., Congress, Senate, Committee on Banking, Housing, and Urban Affairs, *Oversight on the Administration of the Housing and Community Development Act of 1974*, 94th Cong., 2nd sess., 23-26 August 1976, p. 11 (hereafter Senate, *CDBG Oversight*).

34. See summary of research by the General Accounting Office in Senate, *CDBG Oversight*, pp. 540-565.

35. Nathan et al., *Block Grants*, pp. 427-433.

36. U.S., Department of Housing and Urban Development, *Community Development Block Grant Program: First Annual Report* (Washington, D.C.: Government Printing Office, 1975), p. 95 (hereafter HUD, *CDBG—1st Annual Report*).

37. Nathan et al., *Block Grants*, pp. 483-484.

38. HUD, *CDBG—2nd Annual Report*, p. 153.

39. ACIR, *Community Development*, p. 43.

40. See, for example, HUD, *CDBG—2nd Annual Report*, p. 146; and Dale Rogers Marshall and Robert Waste, "Large City Responses to the Community Development Act: A Northern California Study," California Studies in Community Policy and Change, No. 2 (Davis: Institute of Governmental Affairs, Univ. of California, 1977), p. 20.

41. U.S., Congress, House, Committee on Banking, Finance and Urban Affairs, Subcommittee on Housing and Community Development, *Community Development Block Grant Program: Staff Report*, 95th Cong., 1st sess., February 1977, p. 9 (hereafter House, *CDBG—Staff Report*).

42. As quoted in Nathan et al., *Block Grants*, p. 68.

43. HUD, *CDBG—1st Annual Report*, p. 15; and HUD, *CDBG—2nd Annual Report*, p. 127.

44. See, for example, House, *CDBG—Staff Report*, p. 32; and Nathan et al., *Block Grants*, p. 63.

45. House, *CDBG—Staff Report*, p. 46.

46. Dommel et al., *Decentralizing Community Development*, p. 75; and U.S., Department of Housing and Urban Development, Program Planning and Evaluation, Region IX, *Community Development Block Grant Program: Third Survey of Entitlement Cities* (mimeo, May 1977), pp. 23-24 (hereafter HUD, *Region IX Survey*).

47. *City of Hartford* v. *Carla Hills et al.*, Memorandum of Decision, U.S., Court, District of Connecticut, Civil No. H-75-258.

48. Dommel et al., *Decentralizing Community Development*, p. 95.

49. ACIR, *Community Development*, pp. 38, 54.

50. U.S., Congress, Senate, Committee on Banking, Housing, and Urban Affairs, *Oversight on the Progress of the Programs of the Department of Housing and Urban Development During the Year 1977*, 95th Cong., 2nd sess., 27 January 1978, p. 12 (hereafter Senate, *HUD Oversight*).

51. ACIR, *Community Development*, p. 39.

52. Michigan Advisory Commission to the U.S. Commission on Civil Rights, *Civil Rights and the Housing and Community Development Act of 1974, Volume II: A Comparison with Model Cities* (Washington, D.C.: Government Printing Office, 1976), pp. 14-15.

53. House, *CDBG—Staff Report*, p. 6.

54. Francine F. Rabinovitz, Jeffrey L. Pressman, and Martin Rein, "Guidelines: A Plethora of Forms, Authors, and Functions," *Policy Sciences* 7 (1976):400.

55. ACIR, *Community Development*, pp. 37-38; and Stanfield, "The Latest Community Development Flap—Targeting on the Poor," p. 1878.

56. Senate, *CDBG Oversight*, p. 505.

57. Representative Garry Brown (R.-Mich.), as quoted in "House Stings HUD in Anti-Legislative Veto Vote on Bill," *National Journal Reports* 10 (1978):1099.

58. ACIR, *Community Development*, p. 42.

59. HUD, *CDBG—2nd Annual Report*, p. 123.

60. Dommel et al., *Decentralizing Community Development*, pp. 102, 106.

61. Nathan et al., *Block Grants*, p. 383.

62. Senate, *CDBG Oversight*, pp. 3-5; and ACIR, *Community Development*, pp. 23-24.

63. Dommel et al., *Decentralizing Community Development*, pp. 112, 113, 134; and Nathan et al., *Block Grants*, p. 494.

64. Nathan et al., *Block Grants*, p. 488.

65. Ibid., pp. 424-425.

66. Ibid., p. 444.

67. Dommel et al., *Decentralizing Community Development*, pp. 82-83.

68. Ibid., p. 69.

69. House, *CDBG—Staff Report*, p. 5.

70. HUD, *CDBG—1st Annual Report*, p. 30.

71. Dommel et al., *Decentralizing Community Development*, p. 171.

72. U.S., Department of Housing and Urban Development, *Community Development Block Grant Program: Third Annual Report* (Washington, D.C.: Government Printing Office, 1978), p. 230 (hereafter HUD, *CDBG—3rd Annual Report*).

73. Ibid., p. 202.

74. Dommel et al., *Decentralizing Community Development*, pp. 171, 174-188.

75. Ibid., p. 12.

76. Ibid., p. 86.

77. ACIR, *Community Development*, p. 71.

78. Bernard J. Frieden and Marshall Kaplan, "Community Development and the Model Cities Legacy," Working Paper No. 42 (Joint Center for Urban Studies of the Massachusetts Institute of Technology and Harvard University, mimeo, 1976), p. 30.

79. Nathan et al., *Block Grants*, pp. 242-243.

80. Ibid., p. 242.

81. Dommel et al., *Decentralizing Community Development*, p. 183.

82. Ibid., p. 191; Senate, *CDBG Oversight*, p. 3; ACIR, *Community Development*, pp. 62-63; and Nathan et al., *Block Grants*, p. 242.

83. House, *CDBG—Staff Report*, pp. 11-13; HUD, *Region IX Survey*, pp. 6-9; Nathan et al., *Block Grants*, pp. 197-198; and Dommel et al., *Decentralizing Community Development*, p. 238.

84. House, *CDBG—Staff Report*, p. 11; and Senate, *CDBG Oversight*, p. 3.

85. ACIR, *Community Development*, p. 50.

86. HUD, *CDBG—1st Annual Report*, p. 31.

87. House, *CDBG—Staff Report*, p. 3; Nathan et al., *Block Grants*, pp. 484-487.

88. Dommel et al., *Decentralizing Community Development*, p. 203.

89. ACIR, *Community Development*, p. 14.

90. For an excellent discussion of the sociospatial approach and some of the problems associated with it see Sarah F. Liebschutz, "Community Development Block Grants: Who Benefits?" Paper delivered at the 1977 Annual Meeting of the American Political Science Association, Washington, D.C., 1-4 September 1977; and Raymond A. Rosenfeld, "National and Local Performance in Community Development Block Grants: Who Benefits?" Paper delivered at the 1978 Annual Meeting of the American Political Science Association, New York, New York, 31 August-3 September 1978.

91. For a thorough discussion of HUD's method see HUD, *CDBG—3rd Annual Report*, pp. 52-63 and Appendix E.1.

92. National Association of Housing and Rehabilitation Officers, *Newsletter* 11 (3 January 1977).

93. Nathan et al., *Block Grants*, p. 308.

94. Ibid., p. 309.

95. Ibid., pp. 321-324.

96. U.S., Department of Housing and Urban Development, *Community Development Block Grant Program Urban Counties: The First Year Experience* (Washington, D.C.: Government Printing Office, 1977), p. 34.

97. HUD, *CDBG—3rd Annual Report*, p. 252.

98. Rufus P. Browning, Dale Rogers Marshall, and David H. Tabb, "Implementation and Political Change: Sources of Local Variations in Federal Social Programs," paper delivered at the Workshop on Policy Implementation, Pomona College, Pomona, Calif., 16-17 November 1978, pp. 19-20.

99. HUD, *CDBG—2nd Annual Report*, p. 37.

100. HUD, *CDBG—3rd Annual Report*, p. 443.

101. Senate, *CDBG Oversight*, p. 3; see also Nathan et al., *Block Grants*, p. 331; Dommel et al., *Decentralizing Community Development*, p. 244; and House, *CDBG—Staff Report*, p. 12.

102. Nathan et al., *Block Grants*, p. 129.

103. House, *CDBG—Staff Report*, p. 21.

104. Dommel et al., *Decentralizing Community Development*, p. 20.

105. ACIR, *Community Development*, p. 64.

106. For a good discussion of HUD's role see Rosenfeld, "National and Local Performance in Community Development Block Grants."

107. Senate, *CDBG Oversight*, p. 513.

108. See, for example, Liebschutz, "Community Development Block Grants," p. 24; Nathan et al., *Block Grants*, p. 318; Dommel et al., *Decen-*

tralizing Community Development, pp. 87-91; and, for a different view, Marshall and Waste, "Large City Responses to the Community Development Act," p. 13.

109. Dommel et al., *Decentralizing Community Development*, p. 99.

110. House, *CDBG—Staff Report*, pp. 23-24.

111. Senate, *HUD Oversight*, pp. 14-15.

112. "HUD Threatens Cities with Cut-off of Funds If They Neglect Low-Income Housing," *New York Times*, 8 March 1977, p. 14.

113. See, for example, Iver Peterson, "Suffolk County Is Resisting Public Housing Rise," *New York Times*, 25 April 1977, pp. 33, 57.

114. See, for example, Stanfield, "The Latest Community Development Flap—Targeting on the Poor," pp. 1877-1879.

115. "Cities Win More Say on HUD Grants," *Congressional Quarterly Weekly Report* 36 (1978):3218.

116. HUD, *CDBG—3rd Annual Report*, p. 82.

117. Liebschutz, "Community Development Block Grants," p. 26.

118. Dommel et al., *Decentralizing Community Development*, p. 203.

119. Browning, Marshall, and Tabb, "Implementation and Political Change," pp. 20-22.

120. Nathan et al., *Block Grants*, p. 325.

121. Browning, Marshall, and Tabb, "Implementation and Political Change," p. 23.

122. House, *CDBG—Staff Report*, p. 11.

123. See, for example, Nathan et al., *Block Grants*, pp. 315, 319.

124. Senate, *CDBG Oversight*, p. 4.

125. See, for example, House, *CDBG—Staff Report*, p. 36; Marshall and Waste, "Large City Responses to the Community Development Act," pp. 23-24; Nathan et al., *Block Grants*, p. 484; and Dommel et al., *Decentralizing Community Development*, pp. 112-113, 203.

126. Nathan et al., *Block Grants*, pp. 309, 460.

5

Patterns of Policy Implementation: Implications for Intergovernmental Policy and American Politics

Implementing public policy in the American federal system is a complex, dynamic, frustrating, and bewildering task—difficult even when people agree on policy goals.[1] Bureaucratic routine holds sway over participants, delaying reformist policies and deflecting them into the familiar way of doing things.[2] And if policies are difficult to implement when goals are agreed upon, resources are abundant, and priorities are clear, then they are surely even more difficult to carry out when goals are ambiguous, discord among federal, state, and local officials is high, and time and knowledge about how to proceed are inadequate.

Over a five- to seven-year period, thousands of state and local governments delivered over $100 billion of federal aid to millions of people through revenue sharing, CETA, and the community development programs. With all the institutions and actors, the huge sums of money, and the ambiguities in the laws' goals, one might wonder how anything worked at all. Yet patterns and general trends emerge that help us grasp the complexities of the process. This concluding chapter brings together observations about the three laws and paints in broad, sometimes rapid brush strokes a landscape of American politics, public policy design, and the process of implementing intergovernmental programs.

Who Governs?

The New Federalism policies—General Revenue Sharing, the Comprehensive Employment and Training Act (CETA), and Community Development Block Grants—attempted to reshape the distribution of power in the American political system.[3] The laws decentralized authority for designing and running programs from the federal bureaucracy to governors, mayors, and county executives in state and local governments. Authority was centralized with state and local elected officials in general purpose governments.[4]

Elected Officials and Citizen Participation

Elected officials were more centrally involved in making decisions about the nature of employment and training programs and community development strategies than they were during the categorical period when federal grant-in-aid programs bypassed city halls and county courthouses. General Revenue Sharing, in contrast, generated few departures from normal practices of local decision-making. Because state and local officials dominate government budgetary processes, they continued to control the distribution of general aid money from the revenue sharing program.

Indeed, the context of decision-making under CETA and the community development program differed significantly from the environment of General Revenue Sharing. During the categorical era, manpower and community development programs were operated by private, nonprofit organizations such as Community Action Agencies or quasi-public agencies such as Community Development or Urban Renewal authorities. Established by federal legislators to carry out the national government's grant initiatives, these paragovernments planned and operated federal programs in states and localities, making only fleeting contacts with elected political authorities in their jurisdictions.[5] Though such agencies were not shut out of CETA and the Community Development Act, the laws reversed the flow of resources and power away from them and enlarged the role and power of generalist elected officials.

Ironically, by centralizing program authority with mayors and county executives, the laws handed to local chief elected officials power over federal program funds that they often did not have over revenues raised and spent within their political jurisdictions.[6] Most city and county executives share power over locally developed programs with legislatures and other independently elected officials. But the federal legislation created the politically troubling specter of elected officials administering CETA and community development funds in cities and counties where they have no equivalent authority over local programs. In such circumstances, accountability for program decisions was not increased by the enlarged role of chief elected officials, but muddled further.

Though elected officials were more intimately involved in making choices about how to apply federal funds, they concentrated on making decisions with the highest political consequences—allocating program funds among competing organizations and interests and distributing funds directly related to the provision of local government services. Choices affecting who gets what at the expense of whom command the attention of political executives. Less politically charged questions, such as the programs' designs, were delegated to professional staffs.

A central argument made on behalf of decentralizing program control to local elected officials was that the community's citizenry would then have greater opportunities to influence the application of federal funds than they could have over federal administrators or community-based, private organizations.[7] It was further suggested that, because elected officials could be held accountable at the ballot box, they would be more responsive than Washington's bureaucrats to local needs and interests. In various ways, the three laws bow to this philosophical tenet by encouraging citizen participation in the design and administration of the programs.

The lofty aspirations for increased local accountability through active citizen participation were not achieved under General Revenue Sharing or the manpower programs and only partially approached under the Community Development programs. Interest and participation in the New Federalism programs did not extend much beyond the traditional boundaries of normally active individuals and organizations in the local political process. Participating individuals tended to represent vested interests fighting for organizational survival. The programs seldom entered the agenda for debate during election campaigns.

Experience under the three laws varied widely, but the community development programs seemed to generate the greatest amount of citizen interest and activity: neighborhood groups that had heretofore not participated in shaping community development programs were drawn into the process. But organizations nurtured by federal categorical programs successfully competed with them for influence and funds. Citizen participation in employment and training programs was less notewothy because most manpower planning councils were stacked with government officials and agency representatives, holdovers from the categorical period. Community involvement in the revenue sharing program resembled patterns characteristic of the state and local governments' regular budgetary processes.

Factors identified in the model of intergovernmental policy implementation help account for these broad patterns of participation by elected officials and citizens. The statutes placed state and local elected officials at the pinnacle of program decision-making, thus creating a flow of power to these officials. Legislative mandates for citizen involvement, in contrast, were weak and ambiguous. The initial revenue sharing law required no mechanism for capturing citizen views. CETA established manpower planning councils as its citizen participation vehicle; CDBG called for public hearings. But, ironically, the laws upheld the authority of elected officials to control the citizen participation process—who participates, when, and under what circumstances. And the laws did not require representation of potential program beneficiaries, such as the poor and minorities. In short, by letting local officials manipulate the citizen participation process, the laws effectively undermined the independent force that citizens could have exercised over mayors and county officials.[8]

In *reauthorizing* General Revenue Sharing, CETA, and the Community Development Act, Congress incrementally bolstered citizen participation provisions but preserved the central role of elected officials. Congress responded to the demands of national interest groups seeking stronger citizen participation clauses in the laws without alienating state and local elected officials who opposed unfettered citizen input. Whether the adjustments in citizen participation requirements will make any impact remains to be seen, but as long as elected officials determine the nature of that participation, changes are likely to be marginal.

Federal administering agencies basically ignored local decision-making processes under the three laws. While their policy was certainly in tune with the general philosophy of the New Federalism and the autonomy of state and local governments, it also attests to the insignificance that federal agencies attached to the citizen participation goals of the laws.

Given statutory flexibility by Congress and inattention by federal agencies, the local policy environment principally determined governance patterns for the three laws. The attitudes of local elected officials toward their role and the role of external groups were critical. When elected officials assumed active management of the programs, citizen participation usually diminished. Citizen participation became more important when uninterested politicians created a natural power vacuum which others could fill. Citizen groups occasionally acted as political buffers for elected officials, helping to make and legitimize difficult and unpopular choices. Under CETA, for example, manpower planning councils often handled such difficult choices as which applicants would receive CETA contracts or which organization would get CETA-funded public service employees. Even in these situations, elected officials retained veto power over the councils' choices.

But political officials did not always control and orchestrate the involvement of citizen groups. In some cities and counties individuals and groups outside the governmental structure significantly influenced the priorities of revenue sharing, manpower, and community development programs. The vast resources funneled into comunities through the three laws stimulated the involvement of a wide range of interests.

Organizations that prospered during the categorical era worked to preserve their predominant role in delivering manpower and community development programs. Individuals and agencies previously excluded from reaping federal largess viewed the new programs as another opportunity to stake claims and grab a piece of the action. The resulting political environment was often troublesome to manage as elected officials found themselves arbitrating disputes among multiple, competing interests.

While local elected officials gained authority for making New

Federalism program choices, they also inherited the political liabilities associated with that authority. It is therefore understandable why many elected officials decided to let their staffs and community groups fight with one another over the distribution of program funds, thus removing themselves from a political hotseat.

It is also understandable why program specialists and vested interest groups continued to dominate decisions on the details of program design. As Carl Stenberg of the Advisory Commission on Intergovernmental Relations observed,

> We ignore . . . the basic fact of life—that local government is a part-time government. For example, we want to place the mayor in the driver's seat. Yet, this person puts in eight hours at the florist shop and then goes over to city hall and reviews and acts on the community development plan. . . . It's unrealistic to expect this person to make a major commitment of his or her free time, if there is any left after all these meetings, to do the home work really necessary to be in the driver's seat for such complex programs and not just be a figurehead. I think that block grant programs subscribe to what someone once called, "the myth of the generalists." The real power holders are still the specialists, and I would suspect that you will find the same thing with respect to citizen participation.[9]

Elected officials and the average citizen just don't have the time or the interest to get deeply involved in revenue sharing, community development, or manpower programs, except in the most pressing circumstances.

One pressing circumstance that could draw elected officials into New Federalism program minutiae was a budgetary short fall. States, cities, and counties under strong financial pressures often used revenue sharing, CETA, and the community development program funds to help bridge their jurisdictions' fiscal depressions. During such crises, the New Federalism programs received lavish attention from elected officials and their advisors, but local citizen groups had little input about program allocations. Critical choices were made by political officials. When fiscal problems were less acute or nonexistent, elected officials could afford to be uninterested in the programs; opportunities for citizen participation were enhanced. Allocating scarce resources under fiscal pressure was a process dominated by political elites. When budget decisions were less critical, decision-making was more open and involved wider segments of the community.

Varying patterns of governance under the three laws raise an important question about the three policies. Why were politics and citizen participation under the Community Development Act more intense and widespread than under CETA or General Revenue Sharing? Differences among the policies may be accounted for by the histories of the programs and the nature of the policies themselves.

First, the three programs had different histories of local citizen participation upon which to build. Community development programs inherited the legacy of extensive participation fostered by the Model Cities program. Manpower programs had no equivalent citizen participation during the categorical era, and revenue sharing had no history.

Second, the approaches to citizen participation mandated by CETA and CDBG and ignored in revenue sharing's statute produced different outcomes. At first glance, CETA's institutionalized manpower planning councils would appear to have the greatest potential for promoting active citizen involvement. But the manpower planning councils' membership was selected by chief elected officials and the law encouraged representation from groups that had operated categorical manpower programs. These conditions significantly affected the kind of participation emanating from the councils. Generally, manpower planning councils were controlled by the elected officials or their staffs; the members worked on preserving the status quo and their organization's role in it. In contrast, citizen participation in community development programs funneled through public hearings was less predictable and manageable from the standpoint of the elected officials. Public hearings attracted new groups into the process of determining community development programs.[10]

Third, and most important, CDBG decision-making became more intense and visible than that of CETA and General Revenue Sharing because of the program's potential impact on communities. In order to appreciate this point it is helpful to consider the concepts of "distributive" and "redistributive" policy, developed by Theodore Lowi.[11] According to Lowi, different political processes are associated with public policies, depending on the nature of the policy's potential impact on the distribution of benefits in society. Because redistributive policies, such as welfare programs, transfer resources from the haves to the have-nots, they are more visible to the public and generate higher degrees of political conflict among groups. Distributive policies, or classic pork-barrel programs such as rivers and harbors legislation or agricultural subsidies, reward a particular block of people without ostensibly harming other segments of society. Winners and losers are not sharply identified; everyone seems to benefit. Such policies are characterized by bargaining and compromise among participants in the political process.

CDBG and CETA were potentially redistributive because they expressed national goals for serving disadvantaged groups in society and thus might transfer income and benefits to them. Revenue sharing was a distributive program because all classes of citizens could benefit from it. Virtually any type of program could be funded no matter what income group it benefited. Thus the politics of allocating the state or local shared revenues caused less conflict and involved fewer interest groups: the stakes of the game were lower and passions were less aroused among participants. Why did community development programs create more interest group participation and political squabbling than CETA?

CETA's programs were less noticeable and less threatening to the social and political environment of communities in which they were implemented than community development programs. Both statutes contained redistributive rhetoric in the form of mandates for service to disadvantaged members of communities, but, in practice, CDBG's redistributive potential raised more concern among the local citizenry. CETA provided training programs and temporary low-wage employment for unemployed and low-income people. Through such programs, CETA's participants could become "productive," taxpaying members of society, and welfare roles could be reduced. Even if CETA programs enrolled high proportions of low-income people and minorities, the intent of moving such individuals into unsubsidized employment was endorsed by people occupying widely different positions on the liberal-conservative spectrum. Though the issue of public service employment programs once deeply divided liberals and conservatives, Democrats and Republicans, by the late 1970s the role of the federal government in guaranteeing jobs was no longer as controversial. A poll conducted by the Eagleton Institute of Politics of Rutgers University in early 1979 found, for example, that 73 percent of New Jersey's residents agreed that the federal government should fund large-scale public service jobs programs in periods of high unemployment.[12]

While CDBG was also aimed at the low- or moderate-income individual, its program impacts could affect the general living environment in much more direct ways than CETA's. Community development programs, such as public housing construction and rent subsidies, could alter patterns of racial integration, and therefore were often viewed as threatening to middle- and upper-income areas, schools, and property values. Issues such as racial integration and equal housing opportunity stimulated more passionate responses from residents than the question of what types of people obtained public service employment under CETA. The impact of a CETA program that hires a large number of minorities was less immediate than the impact of public housing units located in middle-income neighborhoods. CDBG's programmatic consequences were often expressed in bricks and mortar.

Congress ignores the redistributive implications of public policy when it can. Thus, according to Randall Ripley and Grace Franklin, CETA's redistributive potential was "fuzzed over by the use of a formula to allocate funds and by the stress on local control."[13] But the redistributive aspects of community development programs were more difficult for Congress to avoid, making them more visible to the public and the media and grabbing the attention of elected officials more quickly than CETA.

The reauthorization histories of CETA and the Community Development Act confirm the notion that they were viewed in different ways by national elected officials. Because CETA was in a sense silently redistributive, the eligibility requirements of the law received less congressional scrutiny and interest group comment than the low- and moderate-income targeting provisions of the Community Development Block Grant. In part because of this essential difference between the laws, it was politically feasible for Congress to restrict participation in CETA programs in 1978 to long-term unemployed and low-income individuals. Though provisions that would have increased benefits to low- and moderate-income groups were also proposed for the community development program and endorsed by the Carter administration, they were rejected by Congress. The law was revised, however, to channel more money to the distressed inner cities of the Northeast and Middle-west. But this provision did not pass without considerable wrangling and is also less significant than the new targeting provisions of CETA.

The Federal Role

The New Federalism laws reduced the power of federal agencies over the design and administration of federal grants, but the statutes outlined important federal oversight responsibilities. Analysis of the federal role under the three laws reveals a common pattern. Initially, federal agencies assumed a low profile, permitting a high degree of discretion in local decision-making and concentrating on noncontroversial tasks such as collecting information about the programs. Federal officials engaged in relatively little second-guessing of local decisions. Over time, federal agencies shifted to a more aggressive and intrusive stance, more rigorously enforcing existing procedural requirements and giving direction on the substance of local programs.

Reauthorizations of all three laws uniformly increased the statutory provisions for federal monitoring and evaluation of state and local decisions. In the eyes of Congress, the Department of Housing and Urban Development (HUD) overstepped acceptable norms by telling local officials that they had to spend at least 75 percent of their community development funds on low- and moderate-income people. Congress explicitly restrained HUD from engaging in such aggressive behavior. Nevertheless, all the federal administering agencies significantly increased their activity and influence over New Federalism programs during the period under study, even before the statutes were adjusted to authorize an enlarged federal role.

Several factors account for the nature of federal implementation efforts under the laws. The statutes and legislative histories did not establish clear direction for federal implementors. Federal agencies occupied an awkward position, because the laws outline a high degree of flexibility for state and local officials while at the same time insisting on federal enforcement of broad procedural and substantive goals. Because of the ambiguity, if not the contradiction, contained in the statutes, Congress and interest groups desiring either more or less federal intervention attacked the federal administering agency for failure to uphold the law no matter what the agency's interpretation of the legislation.

If federal agencies were aggressive in carrying out their responsibilities, as in the case of HUD under Secretary Harris, some members of Congress and representatives of state and local governments accused them of overstepping statutory authority. If they failed to gain compliance from state and local governments on controversial issues, such as nondiscrimination, the federal agency was assailed by liberal members of Congress and civil rights organizations. Each agency experienced cross-pressures from divergent legislators on Capitol Hill, from state and local governments, and from civil rights groups and categorical program operators.

Federal administrators not only had to contend with these sorts of pressures, but also had to deal with the tension within their agencies between the roles they had played under the categorical system and the new roles outlined for them under CETA and CDBG. For instance, the Departments of Labor and HUD were cast in the unfamiliar role of providing technical assistance to state and local governments while simultaneously acting as federal policemen of the laws' objectives and requirements. Neither agency had much relevant experience for their technical assistance assignment or for the task of overseeing state and local governments. It is therefore understandable that federal agencies tended to assume low-key postures initially.

Inevitably, within a few months after the laws got underway, state and local governments were accused of abuse, mismanagement, and incompetence. Such allegations gave members of Congress and interest groups yearning for a stronger federal presence a platform on which to renew their demands for more concerted enforcement efforts. A familiar scenario was often observed. Federal agency directors were summoned to Capitol Hill to answer charges of administrative ineptitude or state and local government abuses contained in a congressional committee report or General Accounting Office investigation. A stern lecture was delivered by the House or Senate subcommittee chairman about the importance of federal monitoring.

Unfortunately, federal implementing agencies did not always make differential responses to state and local governments. They failed to recognize that some state and local jurisdictions require careful oversight and assistance, while others don't, because they will implement sound, locally developed policies in accord with national objectives. Federal administrators often used a blunderbuss approach to punishing state and local governments for the mistakes of a relatively small number of communities.

When federal agencies commit this error they are engaging in the "Alabama syndrome," so named because drafters of the Economic Opportunity Act (developed in the mid-1960s) excluded all governors from participation in the program because they did not want Alabama Governor George Wallace to have any power over the poverty programs funded by the law.[14] The Alabama syndrome distorts federal program administration because enforcement efforts are carried out with the lowest common denominator in mind. The least effective and most recalcitrant city or state receives the same treatment, the same reporting requirements and program regulations, as the most competent and progressive ones. Federal administrators often feel compelled to behave in this manner in order to reduce the probability that scandals will embarrass them in Congress, but such behavior creates unnecessary dislocations for state and local governments that do not need or deserve such heavy-handed federal monitoring. In the long run, overly detailed and restrictive federal mandates undermine the authority of federal agencies as well, because state and local officials become skilled at circumventing federal restrictions and skeptical and resentful of federal agency guidelines and directives.[15]

Insight into Congress's role in policy implementation emerges from the analysis of the three laws. Congressmen's attempts to shape public policy do not cease when a bill becomes a law. Representatives and senators who have taken a strong interest in the bill during its legislative development press federal agencies to administer the law in accordance with their original policy preferences, even if they weren't incorporated in the final legislation. Senator William Proxmire, for example, harried administrators in the Department of Housing and Urban Development to carry out his interpretation of the Community Development Act's goals for lower-income people.

Eugene Bardach has written approvingly of the legislator who fixes the implementation process by constantly intervening to make sure that the law's mandates are adhered to.[16] The New Federalism laws had a number of "fixers," but they also had what might be called "foulers," namely, legislators who ignored the majority will of the legislative process and substituted their own biases and policy preferences for those contained in the public laws, thus breaking the rules of the game.

Continuing congressional influence over policy implementation may be expressed in various ways, ranging from a congressman's intervention on behalf of local governments in his congressional district to systematic oversight and appropriations hearings, and constant intervention tantamount to administering the program from Capitol Hill. Because federal program administrators must be constantly mindful of the attitudes and actions of key congressional actors such as subcommittee and committee chairmen, it is difficult to overestimate the influence that these legislators have in shaping the federal role in policy implementation. The influence of Congress was no doubt heightened by the ambiguity in the statutes—a condition that invited sustained efforts to bring the federal role into sharper focus.

The fact that congressmen enjoy considerable influence over the administration of federal programs helps account for their willingness to delegate broad administrative authority to federal agencies and even to state and local elected officials. If a congressman really wants to influence the direction of public policy, he will have ample opportunity to exercise his preferences later, after the formal policymaking stage. In fact, a crafty legislator may prefer loosely worded policy enactments by the Congress so that his personal influence will be heightened; for, the vaguer the policy, the more he can mold the outcomes to his liking, a point to which I shall return below.

Another significant point about the federal role in policy implementation is that Congress, national interest groups, and, most certainly, federal officials overestimate the influence that federal regulations and directions have on state and local government actions. National political actors and administrators often act as if they believe that the federal government can easily manipulate state and local government officials to carry out the dictates of the federal government. The evidence on the limits of federal influence presented in this volume reveals the falseness of that image of the federal system.

In fact, the local policy environment, the attitudes and conditions found in state and local government jurisdictions, are much more important in accounting for the use and distribution of program funds than actions by federal-level administrators. Yet these attitudes and conditions are largely beyond the control of federal agencies, especially if local views run contrary to federal preferences. Politically autonomous units of state and local government are seldom intimidated by federal regulations or the orders of federal officials, unless those officials take radical enforcement steps, such as withdrawing program funds—a technique that is rarely employed because it embarrasses both the state or local government and the federal agency.

Policymakers must keep their image of the federal government's influence in proper perspective lest their misperceptions contribute to bad public policy. Because national political officials, program administrators, journalists, and academically based analysts focus so much of their energies and attention on finding out what is happening in Washington, D.C., and federal agencies, they often come to believe that all the important battles of public policy are won and lost in the Capital. This myopia and parochialism lead these individuals to concentrate on perfecting the federal administrative process and to ignore the fact that policy is reshaped and carried out by state and local bureaucrats and elected officials whose influence over program performance is far more significant than the federal government's. This does not mean that national goals and resources or federal administrative agencies are insignificant; to the contrary, they exert considerable influence. But it does mean that the influence and importance of the policies and practices of federal agencies have been mistakenly overemphasized by national policymakers and independent policy analysts.

Finally, it is worth noting that the experience under all three New Federalism laws reaffirms the importance of national political turnovers in presidential administrations. The New Federalism policies were developed and initially implemented by the administrations of Richard Nixon and Gerald Ford. Though they became somewhat more assertive toward state and local governments over time, federal administrators embraced the philosophy of high state and local discretion. Senior administrators swept into office by Jimmy Carter's election to the presidency staked out very different positions, leading their agencies in new directions. Most strikingly, the Department of Housing and Urban Development, under Secretary Harris, took an aggressive posture toward state and local governments, demanding shifts in program emphasis and insisting on more federal control and evaluation. While these are predictable partisan reactions to eight years of Republican rule, they also highlight the different constituencies that administrations can and do represent and how that filters down to the day-to-day administration of public policy.

How Were the Funds Used?

Revenue Sharing, CETA, and the Community Development Act served very different program objectives. General Revenue Sharing supplied general purpose federal aid to state and local governments, with few substantive goals and several procedural strings attached. In contrast, CETA and CDBG emerged from the ruins of haphazardly developed categorical grant-in-aid programs. Heralded as major reform legislation, CETA and the Community Development Act consolidated under block grants only part of the federal human resource and community development policy domains, leaving large segments of federal programs untouched and operating in their traditional manner.

Nevertheless, even the partial reorganization of federal grant programs achieved through the laws enjoyed widespread and strong support from congressmen, presidents, and state and local elected officials. Though participants disagreed with one another over the ideological goals of enhancing state and local government power, they predictably endorsed the managerial goal of program consolidation.[17] The question is what did state and local elected officials do with their newfound authority over programs?

The analysis of General Revenue Sharing showed that states, cities, counties, and townships spent larger proportions of their shared revenues on capital projects, such as equipment purchases and construction, than they spent of locally raised revenues. Local governments allocated very small amounts of revenue sharing monies to social service programs, and substantial sums for public safety and public transportation.

Local government officials achieved minimal reforms in the shape of employment and training programs when authority shifted to them under CETA. By and large most communities funded the same types of employment and training programs, used the same approaches to organizing their human resource programs, and contracted with the agencies that had been funded by the federal government during the categorical era.

Movement away from the categorical program heritage was more pronounced under the Community Development Block Grant. Large-scale, downtown-oriented urban renewal projects, slum clearance and building demolition, and the Model Cities types of social services—the approaches characteristic of the federally managed programs in the two decades before CDBG—declined in significance. In their place, with local elected officials in charge, communities were increasingly funding smaller-scale, short-term public works projects, housing conservation, and rehabilitation.

The components of the model of intergovernmental policy implementation help us understand the record of program reform and expenditures under the New Federalism policies. Overall statutory provisions on the subject of program design and use were very broad, though the Community Development Act offered some moderately clear guidance. The revenue sharing law, for example, stated almost no program use goals, except for the general list of so-called priority expenditures, which apparently had little or no practical effect on local government choices. Employment and training activities authorized by CETA ran the gamut of manpower program approaches at the time of enactment. The Community Development Act authorized a smorgasbord of program approaches, too, but it at least gave program administrators relatively clear encouragement to undertake hardware and capital projects while discouraging the funding of social services. In short, the laws did little to determine the manner in which the $100 billion in federal aid would be used by state and local government officials.

The short lifespan written into the laws by Congress, however, probably influenced local elected officials to spend more of the shared revenues and community development funds on capital projects. Since the programs could be terminated after a few years, drying up the new sources of money, state and local governments often adopted strategies that would yield tangible results: a new government building constructed with revenue sharing funds would endure beyond the law's history regardless of what Congress decided to do.

The prospect for significant reform of local manpower programs was ironically reduced by the massive infusion of public service employment funds under CETA. Staff energies and concern were riveted on building up and then managing the ten-fold expansion in public service jobs: little time was left for the task of revising and improving employment and training programs.

Reauthorizations of CETA and the Community Development Act grafted narrow purpose programs and national goals onto the broad block grants. This phenomenon occurred frequently in CETA, where Congress amended the law several times, inserting categorical programs from youth, veterans, and public service employment. The tendency to recategorize the originally broad purpose grants and make them more specific was less prevalent in CDBG, but an important federally run categorical program directed at the nation's most distressed cities was established in the law's first reauthorization.

Congress apparently adopted the position that, since shared revenues were not traceable, any attempt to restrict program uses was pointless. Thus they removed the priority expenditure requirements when General Revenue Sharing was revised in 1976. Procedural strings, such as the nondiscrimination provisions, were, however, increased to levels in excess of those attached to many categorical grant-in-aid programs of the 1960s.

Federal implementing agencies had little influence over state and local governments' program choices. The Office of Revenue Sharing offered almost no guidance to state and local governments on how to distribute their shared revenues. The Departments of Labor and HUD were somewhat more active, but they did not promote new strategies for employment and training programs or community development. In fact, the Department of Labor occasionally helped categorical program operators maintain their role in manpower delivery systems. HUD reinforced the status quo by insisting that communities finish urban renewal projects started during the years prior to CDBG, thus reducing the funds available for new community development projects.

Ultimately, the local policy environment shaped the use of New Federalism program funds. Of principal importance were the views of chief elected officials about which programs should be funded and which eliminated. For instance, the low level of spending on social services through CDBG and General Revenue Sharing reflected local actors' preferences for programs that do not create a permanent demand for refunding as well as their belief that the laws were not designed to support social services. Moreover, the presence of large quantities of employment and training resources probably reinforced the determination of local officials to steer revenue sharing and community development programs away from social services and into capital projects. CETA funds were mostly restricted to paying enrollees' stipends, wages, or salaries, whereas revenue sharing and community development monies could be used for a variety of other purposes.

The interplay of local interest group politics and citizen participation also influenced program expenditures. For example, under CETA, agencies that had managed federal categorical manpower programs worked through local planning councils and other political channels to hold onto or expand their contracts for employment and training services. Apparently, these community-based organizations have developed sufficient political clout to survive in the local political environment without federal protection because they were usually effective in thwarting attempts to eliminate them.[18] Public hearings and other forums for citizen participation launched by local CDBG programs weakened the grasp of agencies that dominated the categorical era of community development programs. Neighborhood groups demanding services for areas extending beyond the Model Neighborhoods persuaded local elected officials to spread resources to wider segments of the community. Finally, the low-key politics of General Revenue Sharing insured that the state or local governments' dominant coalition would decide how to spend shared revenues.

Local fiscal conditions also influenced the application of New Federalism funds. Fiscally hard-pressed communities and states often folded their shared revenues into the regular budget and used them for tax abatement or stabilization purposes. Larger numbers of CETA-funded public service employees were hired to staff jobs within political jurisdictions experiencing financial difficulties. And cities and counties with the greatest needs applied their community development funds in as many locations as possible, addressing many problems simultaneously.

In shaping the use of program funds, objective measures of need were less important than the general orientations of political decision-makers, their perceptions of economic problems, and their responses to political pressures. Economic and social factors established wide parameters within which programs were planned and operated.

The patterns of program expenditures and reform raise critical issues about national goals and local implementors. National policymakers placed a heavy management burden on local governments when they authorized CETA and the Community Development Act. As one observer put it, "One cannot escape the disquieting notion that [CETA and CDBG constitute] a passing of the coordination buck to localities, after unsuccessful attempts to deal with it in Washington.''[19] Having created a bewildering maze of federally funded programs operated by paragovernments, the New Federalism legislation instructed state and local officials to clean up the categorical mess. By mandating that state and local governments establish "viable urban communities," and "comprehensive manpower systems," CDBG and CETA required the attainment of goals that the federal government had not only failed to reach, but, through a patchwork of programs, probably contributed to undermining.

In addition to the management problems associated with the take-over of the categorical system, state and local governments inherited programs that lacked well-established approaches for achieving positive program outcomes. Policy analysts in the government and the academic community, despite several years of experimentation, trial, and error, had not developed adequate knowledge about methods of enhancing the employability of the economically disadvantaged or strategies for halting urban decline. State and local governments were asked to implement policy beyond their capability.[20] Faced with a complicated management task, and without sufficient information about which programs work under what conditions, it is little wonder that the grand aspirations of the policies were not acheived, or that program performance fell far short of the rhetoric of reform. Moreover, the tendency of federal policymakers to fault state and local governments for their inept handling of the policies must be viewed with a high degree of skepticism.

Important observations about the federal government's influence are revealed by the analysis of the three laws. Although federal administrative agencies do not significantly affect state and local government decisions about how they will employ General Revenue Sharing, CETA, and Community Development funds, indirect federal influence over subnational government behavior has increased for two reasons. First, procedural requirements, such as nondiscrimination provisions, expanded significantly under the New Federalism programs, putting the federal government in a much more threatening position than it had been before. Auditing, monitoring, and evaluation requirements subjected state and local governments to close scrutiny by federal bureaucrats as the price of decentralized programs.[21]

Second, largely due to the three laws and the $100 billion in aid they provide, state and local governments have become increasingly dependent upon federal aid.[22] Direct federal assistance to cities grew by a factor of thirteen in the past ten years, going from $941 million in fiscal year 1968 to $42.5 billion in fiscal year 1978.[23] Federal aid represents an increasingly larger precentage of total state and local government expenditures. According to the Advisory Commission on Intergovernmental Relations, "While in fiscal year 1957, direct federal aid equaled only 1.3 percent of locally raised revenues in Buffalo and 2 percent in Cleveland, by fiscal year 1978, it equaled nearly 70 percent in both cities. . . ."[24] The growing dependency of state and local governments places federal administrators and the national government in a very powerful position. Though it is unlikely to occur, sudden withdrawal of federal aid or a portion of it would engender financial chaos in cities such as Buffalo, Cleveland, and Newark, where federal aid has helped to postpone bankruptcy.

State and local government officials fear that the federal government has fostered this dependency relationship so that it can exert stronger control over its wards. In fact, some state and local officials believe that the New Federalism policies were designed to trick state and local governments and, as such, have perpetrated a cruel hoax. These people argue that the New Federalism policies were sold to state and local governments by a Republican president under the banner of local control and determination. State and local officials responded reluctantly and then enthusiastically to this idea. As soon as they became highly dependent on federal funds, a Democratic president and Congress revised the statutes, making them more restrictive, inserting additional grant conditions and demanding stronger federal oversight. Programs that initially served broad purposes and were loosely administered from Washington, D.C., gathered specific national goals and aggressive federal administrators. The rebirth of an interventionist federal role, or perhaps recentralization and recategorization, leaves state and local officials "in charge" of programs whose shape they are displeased with, but without whose support they cannot balance their budgets. Even if revenue sharing, CETA, and CDBG do not occupy large proportions of their budgets, the programs and people associated with them are now the responsibility of state and local elected officials: they will pay most of the political consequences if funds are reduced or people are fired.

Who Benefits from the New Federalism Programs?

The question of what income groups and types of people should benefit from General Revenue Sharing, CETA, and the Community Development Act generated a great deal of controversy and debate. Though revenue sharing was not intended as aid for the poor, the extent to which its programs and tax reductions benefited them became one of the liveliest reenactment issues in 1976. CETA's enrollment of minorities and disadvantaged people was frequently on the agenda of national policymakers. Congress gradually amended the law, making entrance requirements more restrictive. Congress, the Department of Housing and Urban Development, and intergovernmental actors engaged in prolonged debates and conflict over the definition of the Community Development Act's low- and moderate-income goals.

All the controversy and discord over benefit distribution came about for two reasons. First, opponents of program decentralization argued that state and local government officials would not adequately serve the politically impotent poor unless forced to do so by federal mandates. They found support for their position in the philosophy of government articulated in the late eighteenth century by James Madison in *The Federalist*, No. X:

> The smaller the society, the fewer probably will be the distinct parties and interests composing it; the more frequently will a majority be found of the same party, and the smaller the compass within which they are placed, the more easily will they concert and execute their plans of oppression. Extend the sphere, and you take in a greater variety of parties and interests; you make it less probable that a majority of the whole will have a common motive to invade the rights of other citizens; or if such a common motive exists, it will be more difficult for all who feel it to discover their own strength, and to act in unison with each other.[25]

Naturally, state and local officials rejected the assertion that they would ignore the least advantaged and demanded the right to determine an appropriate mixture of beneficiaries responsive to the nature of local needs.

Second the development of benefit distribution policy sparked controversy because it touched on fundamental questions, such as where federal resources should be concentrated in society and how program funds could most productively be spent. Attempts to reserve funds for the poor and minorities had redistributive implications and thus provoked enduring debate and divisiveness during both the legislative and program implementation processes.

The Community Development Block Grant and CETA were redistributive in rhetoric, but primarily distributive in fact. Following traditional norms of policymaking, Congress authorized programs that could be viewed as subsidies for broad segments of society, or, to recall Lowi's term, Congress preferred distributive policies. Such programs are "likely to get stronger support from all four congressional groups [House and Senate Democrats and Republicans] than either a program of geographically concentrated subsidy or programs involving the manipulation of social benefits and rewards," according to Randall Ripley.[26] Congress muted the potential redistributive implications of CETA and the Community Development Block Grant by packaging the laws as subsidy programs for state and local governments and by inserting only symbolic reassurances into the law to appease interest groups demanding attention for the disadvantaged.[27] Thus, for example, the original CETA legislation contained language urging state and local governments to enroll only those most in need of employment and training services, but did not require them to put exclusive emphasis on the disadvantaged.

The three laws were of varying benefit to the poor and minorities. General Revenue Sharing—a program not designed to benefit low-income people, but nonetheless evaluated by many interest groups by that standard—provided few substantial, direct benefits to the economically disadvantaged. Indirect benefits for low-income individuals were made available through spending on public safety and transportation, but capital projects and property tax abatement made possible through shared revenues tended to benefit middle- and upper-income groups disproportionately. Because evidence assessing the impact of revenue sharing on the poor is scant, General Revenue Sharing will be set aside at this juncture: the remainder of the section compares CETA and Community Development Block Grants.

In comparison with the categorical programs managed by the federal government in the 1960s and early 1970s, CETA enrolled lower proportions of low-income people, minorities, youth, and those with limited formal education under its training and work experience programs. Proportionally, more low-income people participated in CETA's public service employment programs than in the categorical equivalent, known as the Public Employment Program, but CETA public service employees were older, better educated, and less likely to be minorities than before. Decline in benefits for the less advantaged members of society, as measured by these ascriptive characteristics, occurred, but not dramatically. These downward trends were reversed by the 1978 revision of CETA that targeted all programs on people who could meet the dual test of long-term unemployment and poverty status.

CDBG programs spent roughly three-fifths of their resources in census tracts that reasonably qualify as low- and moderate-income areas. While adequate information comparing CDBG with the categorical period is lacking, it is evident that community development projects have been spread to broader cross sections of the communities in which they operate. More census tracts obtained CDBG funds, and there was less emphasis on the most blighted pockets of the inner city. Transitional areas, those parts of the cities sliding toward severe decline, received greater shares of community development resources than before.

The model of policy implementation highlights factors that explain benefit distribution under CETA and CDBG. Legislators, walking a tightrope between groups demanding clear mandates for the poor and those who wanted no federally imposed restrictions, enacted vague and internally contradictory statutes. Thus, despite rhetorical emphasis on the need to serve the least advantaged people and communities, the laws' funding formulas reduced the share of resources for the communities that had participated in the War on Poverty Programs and spread funds into areas of the country that had previously been excluded from federal aid programs because they were not judged to be in need of them. Inevitably, the shift in the composition of grant recipients and specifically the growing number of suburban communities involved in the programs, brought about different mixtures of people in the CETA and community development programs.

The laws were also ambiguous about how much the poor should receive in comparison with other groups. When the Department of Housing and Urban Development attempted to clarify the ambiguity by defining the Community Development Act's "maximum feasible priority" clause for low-and moderate-income people at 75 percent, Congress reacted by insisting that HUD leave the vague language in the statute alone.

Finally, the contradictory objectives for benefit distribution were written into the laws. The Community Development Block Grant authorized programs that could be developed to eliminate slums and blight, to serve low- or moderate-income groups, and to assist middle-income families to stay in or return to the central city. Language in CETA suggested priority for the long-term unemployed, and those who had the least experience and education. But it also indicated that the recently unemployed should be served, regardless of their education or experience in the labor market, until the law was restructured in 1978 to focus more explicitly on the poor. Effectively implementing one of the multiple conflicting objectives of CETA or the Community Development Act could cancel out the other ones.

Indeed, during the initial years of the laws, the Departments of Labor and HUD paid scant attention to the low-income objectives of the acts. Labor, for example, initiated policies that not only overlooked such issues, but also may have reduced benefits for the poor because its policies encouraged the rapid disposal of public service employment monies. The department pursued the countercyclical mission of CETA—to stimulate the lagging national economy. HUD also resisted the temptation to define acceptable levels of low- and moderate-income benefits that communities should strive for with their community development programs. Instead, emphasis was placed on encouraging the completion of urban renewal projects and on fostering local government control of community development programs.

Under the Carter administration, the departments put more energy into fulfilling the laws' commitment to serve the poor and other disadvantaged groups. The Department of Labor pressured local governments to enroll larger numbers of low-income and long-term unemployed people and advocated amendments to tighten entrance requirements. HUD threatened communities with fund withdrawals if they ignored the needs of their low- and moderate-income residents. In summary, the influence of the federal administering agencies varied from almost none at the beginning to moderate during the Carter years. More important, their postures toward the appropriate benefit patterns were highly inconsistent throughout the implementation process.

The local policy environment was the most important determinant of benefit distribution under CETA and the Community Development Act. Among the factors in the local policy environment, the attitudes of local implementors about who should benefit and the interaction between their positions and local interest group politics were most significant. Many state and local officials did not view CETA or the Community Development Act as poverty programs, but as laws with broad objectives, including service to a cross section of the local community. The politics of citizen participation under the community development programs reinforced these attitudes. Participation by various neighborhood groups, noted above, brought demands for service in areas of the community that had not received funds before. In contrast, the strong community organizations represented on CETA-manpower planning councils occasionally helped to minimize changes in the nature of program enrollees by effectively representing low-income and minority interests.

General program strategies followed under the two laws also help account for patterns of program benefits. The shift toward housing conservation and rehabilitation and away from social services and urban renewal projects allowed local governments to mount small-scale projects in more areas of the community and to redirect them from neighborhoods favored during the categorical era. The huge growth of public service employment programs under CETA meant that its programs would require more preparation, experience, and education of applicants—a factor leading to reductions in service for the disadvantaged.

Local economic and social conditions, and other measures of objective needs, help explain broad community development and employment and training strategies and therefore, indirectly, benefit distribution. Nevertheless, political judgments, such as the desire to reward supportive constituencies and respond to interest group demands, were probably more important in explaining ultimate choices about who benefited from the programs.

Evidence on who benefits from the New Federalism highlights issues concerning redistributive public policies and the efficacy of the intergovernmental system as a vehicle for implementing them. Though it has long been argued in American politics that decentralizing power to state and local governments favors middle- and upper-income groups, the worst fears about single group domination were not realized. Benefits were more widely distributed under CETA and CDBG than they would be under strict targeting requirements, but the outcomes departed less from the categorical patterns than predicted by liberal opponents of decentralization.

Two essential points are often overlooked in the debates over centralization and decentralization. First, national goals favoring the economically disadvantaged were not ignored by all state and local officials. In fact, most of them attempted to implement public policy in good faith and in accordance with clearly stated national objectives. Thus, for example, revisions restricting enrollment in CETA's public service employment programs produced immediate increases in the number of long-term unemployed and low-income participants, as local officials responded to the revised policy standards.

Second, and equally important, interest groups representing the poor and minorities, nurtured by federal grants during the decade of the 1960s, were evidently stronger than some observers predicted and thus were able to retain a large share of community development and CETA funds for the people they represented.[28] One of the important legacies of the War on Poverty was a bolstering of these groups in the local political process. Such groups are now either part of the dominant coalition in their community or a loud enough voice that they usually must be reckoned with.[29]

Combining these two points, it seems that the policy of decentralizing authority for redistributive programs to the local level is a highly desirable approach to policy delivery because national goals favoring the poor are not necessarily sacrificed in the process: there is no necessary tradeoff between the goal of decentralization and the goal of income redistribution or serving the poor.[30] If national policymakers want state and local government officials to implement redistributive policy, however, the laws should be written in such a way as to counter the tendency of some local officials to serve the more advantaged members of those communities. Many communities will not even need strong or clear federal legislation because spokesmen within them will successfully represent the interests of the poor.

The president and Congress can greatly increase the likelihood that lower-income people will benefit from intergovernmental programs by adopting legislation that clearly targets program resources on those people, as was eventually achieved in the 1978 reauthorization of CETA. Though strong incentives normally lead policymakers to avoid the tough decisions about who should benefit from federal programs, leaving this choice to the federal bureaucrats and state and local officials, as most federal legislation does, undermines national goals and creates an uncertain and volatile political environment.

The federal government should reoccupy the role of "scapegoat" for local politicians. By providing strict and clear guidelines on who should be served by federal grants, Congress and the president can relieve state and local officials from taking responsibility for potentially controversial and unpopular decisions.[31] Narrow federal eligibility standards are especially important where the local constituency for a federal program is weak[32] and can actually expand the latitude of state and local officials by providing them with a convenient excuse for not bowing to middle- and upper-income group demands. State and local government officials can abide restrictive federal mandates and may even welcome them, but, when faced with ambiguous rules, they will often opt for the more influential groups in the community. In many communities, despite the significant awakening of groups advocating service for the poor and minorities, the dominant coalition is not composed of disadvantaged individuals.

Conclusion: National Goals and Local Implementors

The foregoing discussion on the advantages of clear federal statutes raises a question woven throughout this entire volume. How important are clear goals to the implementation of public policy? The analysis demonstrates that it is extremely difficult to obtain such policy direction because of the Congress's propensity to enact vague and internally contradictory legislation.

Ambiguous, multiple-purpose legislation has been elevated to an art form by American policymakers. Such policy statements are understandable if one reflects on the American political process and the goals of individuals occupying our elective political offices. The legislative process is characterized by attempts to reconcile the competing claims of interest groups and political theories as well as the divergent preferences of legislators. The resulting compromises mold policy statements into language that majority coalitions can support. The broader the language, and, often, the less redistributive its intent, the larger the group that can reach consensus on the policy. Congressmen shepherding legislation through Capitol Hill strive for policies that satisfy widely different interests. By avoiding explicit policy objectives and delegating the hard choices to federal bureaucracies, Congressmen not only gather more broad-based support for legislation but also give themselves more leeway to blame federal agencies for failures in carrying out legislative intent and take credit for correcting its faults through constituent casework.[33]

The preference for policy ambiguity is strongly reinforced by the congressman's goals. Though congressmen have many personal, policy, and institutional goals, all find it necessary constantly to position themselves in such a way as to enhance their prospects for reelection.[34] Congressmen therefore prefer legislation that appeals to a wide segment of their political constituencies. This fact helps account for both the prevalence of vague national goals and the difficulty of enacting legislation that has clear redistributive implications.

The interests of other participants in the political process are also served by unclear national policy. Despite the problems that such legislation may cause, executive branch agencies often endorse this approach because it provides more administrative flexibility to them. State and local officials also support open-ended policy because they gain additional discretion and freedom from federal interference.

Perhaps the most basic reason producing vague policy is that policymakers usually don't know exactly what they want to achieve, what can be accomplished by government action, or how to do it. Rarely is the knowledge available or the procedures for effectively intervening in society well enough understood that policymakers can confidently establish precise national policy in law. It becomes not only politically convenient, but intellectually necessary to leave some elements of the law undefined and subject to the further refinement by federal, state, and local implementors.

Observing the congressional tendency to authorize vague laws and delegate authority to federal agencies, Henry Friendly, Theodore Lowi, and others have complained that even chaos would be preferable to a bad (that is, ambiguous) law. By their reckoning, national legislators and presidents should only act on those matters where consensus on clear policy statements can be achieved and where the potential consequences of public policy are clearly understood.[35]

I reject that assertion not only because it implies a very short and unambitious public policy agenda, but also because some amount of flexibility or lack of legislative clarity may be necessary for effective implementation. Richard Weatherley and Michael Lipsky concluded their study of special-education reform by commenting:

> Practical men and women charged with carrying out new legislation understandably and correctly seek appropriate resources, clarity in objectives and priorities, and certainty of support. Our analysis has focused on how school personnel respond when these matters are in doubt. But our findings do not mean that social-reform legislation should be limited to mandating only that which street-level personnel can easily accomplish. On the contrary, much would be lost by reducing the scope of legislation to only that which can be readily accommodated. . . . This focus overlooks the role of law in giving legitimacy to conceptions of the social order and in directing people's energies toward objectives even if these objectives cannot be achieved completely in the short run.[36]

Public policies often should be broadly drawn so that federal, state, and local implementors can adapt them to the complexities of the intergovernmental system and to rapid changes in economic and political conditions.

Given the strong political and institutional incentives described above, it is unlikely that Congressmen will suddenly reverse their practices and start passing unambiguous laws. Reform in the development of national policy goals will not occur unless the political process and the behavior of politicians change. There are no strong reasons to suspect that this will happen, and good reasons for wishing that it does not happen.

Though it seems likely that Congress will and should write ambiguous legislation when there is uncertainty about the procedures for producing effective public policy, the analysis presented in this volume underscores the importance of clear national goals when lawmakers seek redistributive outcomes. Scarce resources demand that political officials make hard political choices regarding the most effecient use of national funds. Congress proved that it could accomplish this when it significantly restricted entrance requirements for CETA programs in the 1978 revision of the law. In summary, national policy should be specific about the ends it wishes to achieve, but less specific about the means for achieving those ends, leaving appropriate administrative discretion to state and local government officials for the design of programs suited to their communities' needs.

Unclear public policies and vague national goals, along with the fundamental autonomy that state and local governments enjoy in the federal system, are the principal explanations for the minimal impact that public laws and federal implementing agencies have on intergovernmental policy implementation. This statement may seem anticlimactic, coming as it does after a treatment that offers abundant evidence in support of this claim. Nevertheless, it is important to recall that the image of virtually unbounded federal power, of an uncontrollable federal juggernaut, resides in the minds of many Washington-based policymakers and analysts, members of Congress and the executive branch, and the media. While there is truth to the notion that the fedeal government influences state and local government behavior, this volume demonstrates that its strength can be greatly exaggerated.[37]

In fact, the federal government's influence on state and local government program implementation is often rather limited. David Walker, of the Advisory Commission on Intergovernmental Relations, observes: "The Federal bureaucracy . . . frequently [resembles] a big head with no body. Supervision, monitoring, and assessment of aid programs frequently become less stringent in practice than in principle. The Administrtion and Congressional tendency to institute grant conditions and then to constrain or cut agency manpower is as strong today as it ever was."[38] Federal officials should be less sanguine, if they aren't already, about their ability to mold state and local government behavior. National interest groups should be more attentive to state and local politics and administrative processes. And professional analysts should place less emphasis on national politics and administrative actions in their assessments of public policy. The policy's standards and resources circumscribe state and local action, but public policy happens, succeeds or flops, in thousands of state and local governments and private agencies. Anyone who seeks to influence or understand policy implementation must therefore set his sights on the day-to-day activities at the local level.

Because national goals are generally ambitious, there is usually a wide gap between them and the actual achievement of concrete results. The rhetoric of reform so often repeated in public laws leads Congress, the executive branch, interest groups, and the public to expect major changes and improvement in the delivery of public services. When little improvement is evident, or when results are negative, disillusionment sets in.[39] General Revenue Sharing, CETA, and the Community Development Block Grants were supposed to help reshape methods of policy delivery and improve the management of government programs. In part due to the high expectations, disappointment among some congressional policymakers and federal agency heads was great when evidence of program accomplishments showed few program innovations and signs of mismanagement and incompetence in some communities. Of course, opponents of decentralized public policy seized the disappointing results, exploiting the opportunity to demand legislative revisions and restructuring.

The problem with the reaction of both supporters and detractors of the New Federalism policies is that they were impatient for immediate signs of positive results. Once Congress enacts legislation, usually after months or years of debate, the call for rapid implementation is irresistible. A familiar scenario ensues. The federal agency, pressed for time, struggles to get the program underway. First year results trickle in and complaints multiply. Congressmen, dismayed by the lack of concrete accomplishments and always on the lookout for opportunities to chastise federal officials for inept administration, take steps to amend and overhaul the law. Hostility and disappointment hang over the program like a shroud.

Authorized for relatively short time spans, General Revenue Sharing, CETA, and the Community Development Act had already acquired a large and growing number of critics by the time they were scheduled for reauthorization. Members of Congress and interest group representatives cited evidence of scandal, corruption, and abuse of funds. Familiar themes of government inefficiency and mismanagement were played out in the media. Programs of immense complexity were reduced to simple slogans and trivialized. Thus, for example, *Newsweek* entitled an article on CETA "Jobs and Rip-Offs"; *Reader's Digest*'s title was "CETA: $11 Billion Boondoggle." As the moment approached for reauthorizing the laws, disillusioned former supporters joined longtime opponents in a chorus shouting for funding cutbacks. Nonetheless, the programs survived. How?

The answer lies in the politics of program reauthorization. Though the programs gathered plenty of detractors, they also enjoyed a large and intense coalition of supporters. Various interest groups whose constituencies gained from the programs, federal bureaucrats, and, of course, state and local program administrators and elected officials coalesced to insure that General Revenue Sharing, CETA, and the Community Development Act would survive. The intergovernmental lobby, especially, demonstrated its increasing power over national policymakers, bringing their considerable resources together and burying differences with one another in order to guarantee uninterrupted funding.

Reauthorization politics and congressional oversight of public policy thus tend to wind up tinkering; the outcomes are predictably incremental, unless there is a turnover in the White House, and then more substantial change can be achieved. Congress typically revises the laws just enough to placate interest groups and the public, while simultaneously preserving the fundamental structure of the program, often complete with its shortcomings. Symbolic reassurances were offered in the amendments to the laws, but the statutes were not profoundly altered because the programs had widespread Democratic and Republican support in Congress and the endorsement of the nation's state and local government officials. Movement away from the Republican ideas of the Nixon administration was noticeable, but not radical. The programs were, to say the least, well entrenched on the public policy scene.

Unfortunately, legislators and administrators often fail to analyze the shortcomings of legislation and reshape policy accordingly: the reenactment of General Revenue Sharing, CETA, and the Community Development Block Grant confirm the frequently heard lament that Congress cannot perform and does not want to perform effective oversight of public policy.[40] Morris P. Fiorina describes the workings of the "Washington system":

> By working to establish various federal programs . . . congressmen earn electoral credit from concerned elements of their districts. Some federal agency then takes Congress' vague policy mandate and makes the detailed decisions necessary to translate the legislation into operating programs. The implementation and operation of the programs by the agencies irritate some constituents and suggest opportunities for profit to others. These aggrieved and/or helpful constituents then appeal to their congressmen to intervene. . . . The system is connected when congressmen decry bureaucratic excesses and red tape while riding a grateful electorate to ever more impressive electoral showings.[41]

In short, members of Congress ignore the important issue of program implementation during policy formulation and reauthorization, not because they don't know better, but because it is in their interests to do so.

Although it may seem like a paltry remedy for an intractable problem, I end this volume with a plea for systematic attention to the process of public policy implementation by policymakers, governmental policy analysts, and students of government. Implementing intergovernmental policy is extremely difficult and demanding. More concern must be directed to the long-range development of agency and staff capability at all levels of government for the enormously complicated tasks that they are expected to perform. The president and Congress can foster more effective governmental programs not by simply scaling down the nation's agenda and aspirations, and some observers would have it, but by being more conscious of the consequences of their choices and what they are trying to achieve when they establish national goals.

Analysis of the implementation process can serve an enlightenment function by developing knowledge about effective methods of program delivery, which can be built into the design of public policy and administrative practice. Administrators in federal, state, and local government may avoid the pitfalls of their predecessors by working out "implementation scenarios" that help them anticipate and cope with the delays and diversions so common to intergovernmental policy.[42]

Students of American government can contribute to improving public policy by examining the process and politics of implementation, extending the insights of their disciplines and recording the mistakes of the past so that we don't repeat them again and again. But policy-relevant research will have only marginal impact unless the clients for that research, the policymakers, begin to realize the political imperative of creating and operating better public programs. The alternative, a failure to address the problems of policy implementation, invites further disillusionment in the efficacy of governmental intervention and the legitimacy of representative government.

Notes

1. See Jeffrey L. Pressman and Aaron B. Wildavsky, *Implementation* (Berkeley: Univ. of California Press, 1973), for an example of the problems of implementing policy even when the actors agree on goals.

2. See, for example, Eugene Bardach, *The Implementation Game: What Happens after a Bill Becomes a Law?* (Cambridge, Mass.: MIT Press, 1977), and Graham T. Allison, *Essence of Decision: Explaining the Cuban Missile Crisis* (Boston: Little, Brown and Co., 1971).

3. Jeffrey L. Pressman, "Political Implications of the New Federalism," in Wallace E. Oates, ed., *Financing the New Federalism* (Baltimore: Johns Hopkins Press, 1975), p. 14.

4. Joseph D. Sneed, "Summary of Proceedings," in Joseph D. Sneed and Steven A. Waldhorn, eds., *Restructuring the Federal System: Approaches to Accountability in Postcategorical Programs* (New York: Crane, Russak & Co., 1975), p. 7.

5. The word paragovernments was originated by Daniel F. Moynihan to characterize the nonprofit organizations that ran federal programs during the categorical era; see Daniel F. Moynihan, *Maximum Feasible Misunderstanding: Community Action in the War on Poverty* (New York: Free Press, 1969).

6. George Williams, "Federal Objectives and Local Accountability," in Sneed and Waldhorn, eds., *Restructuring the Federal System*, p. 134.

7. See, for example, Richard P. Nathan, "Special Revenue Sharing," in Sneed and Waldhorn, eds., *Restructuring the Federal System,* p. 38.

8. See Walter A. Rosenbaum, "The Paradoxes of Public Participation," *Administration and Society* 8 (1976):355-382.

9. As quoted in U.S., Advisory Commission on Intergovernmental Relations, *Block Grants: A Roundtable Discussion* (Washington, D.C.: Government Printing Office, 1976), p. 22.

10. On the effectiveness of public hearings see Charles O. Jones, *Clean Air: The Policies and Politics of Pollution Control* (Pittsburgh: Univ. of Pittsburgh Press, 1975); and Daniel A. Mazmanian and Jeanne Nienaber, *Can Organizations Change?: Environmental Protection, Citizen Participation and the Corps of Engineers* (Washington, D.C.: The Brookings Institution, 1979).

11. Theodore J. Lowi, "American Business, Public Policy, Case-Studies, and Political Theory," *World Politics* 16 (1964):677-715.

12. The Eagleton Poll from which this information is drawn was conducted between January 23 and February 2 of 1979 when a random sample of 1,003 New Jersey residents, eighteen years of age or older, were interviewed by telephone. The exact question wording was as follows: Do you think the federal government should provide public jobs for those unemployed who are willing and able to work; or do you think this isn't the government's responsibility?

13. Randall B. Ripley and Grace A. Franklin, *Congress, the Bureaucracy, and Public Policy* (Homewood, Ill.: Dorsey Press, 1976), p. 135.

14. The Alabama syndrome is described in James L. Sundquist, *Making Federalism Work: A Study of Program Coordination at the Community Level* (Washington, D.C.: The Brookings Institution, 1969), p. 271.

15. See, for example, Martha A. Derthick, *The Influence of Federal Grants: Public Assistance in Massachusetts* (Cambridge, Mass.: Harvard Univ. Press, 1970), p. 200.

16. Bardach, *The Implementation Game,* p. 274.

17. See Subcommittee on the Planning Process and Urban Development, Advisory Committee to the U.S. Department of Housing and Urban Development, *Revenue Sharing and the Planning Process: Shifting the Locus of Responsibility for Domestic Problem Solving* (Washington, D.C.: National Academy of Sciences, 1974), pp. 6-7.

18. For an accurate prediction on this subject see Sneed, "Summary of Proceedings," in Sneed and Waldhorn, eds., *Restructuring the Federal System,* p. 11.

19. Roland L. Warren, "Competing Objectives in Special Revenue Sharing," in Sneed and Waldhorn, eds., *Restructuring the Federal System*, pp. 58-59.

20. The phrase "implementing policy beyond capability" is developed in Jones, *Clean Air*, pp. 211-275.

21. For an early discussion of this phenomenon see Nathan, "Special Revenue Sharing," in Sneed and Waldhorn, eds., *Restructuring the Federal System*, pp. 42-43.

22. See, for example, David B. Walker, "A New Intergovernmental System in 1977," *Publius: The Journal of Federalism* 8 (1978):112.

23. Rochelle L. Stanfield, "Federal Aid—Taking the Good with the Bad," *National Journal Reports* 10 (1978):1078.

24. As reported in Rochelle L. Stanfield, "The Development of President Carter's Urban Policy: One Small Step for Federalism," *Publius: The Journal of Federalism* 8 (1978):42.

25. *Federalist Papers*, No. X (New York: New American Library, Mentor, 1961), pp. 60-61.

26. Randall B. Ripley, *The Politics of Economic and Human Resource Development* (Indianapolis: Bobbs-Merrill Co., 1972), p. 165.

27. See Murray Edelman, *The Symbolic Uses of Politics* (Urbana: Univ. of Illinois Press, 1964), p. 23.

28. See Sneed, "Summary of Proceedings," in Sneed and Waldhorn, eds., *Restructuring the Federal System*, p. 11.

29. See, for example, Rufus P. Browning, Dale Rogers Marshall, and David H. Tabb, "Responsiveness to Minorities: A Theory of Political Change in Cities," paper delivered at the 1978 Annual Meeting of the American Political Science Association, New York, New York, 31 August-3 September 1978; and Robert H. Haveman, ed., *A Decade of Federal Antipoverty Programs* (New York: Academic Press, 1977).

30. Warren, "Competing Objectives in Special Revenue Sharing," in Sneed and Waldhorn, eds., *Restructuring the Federal System*, p. 55.

31. For one of many who urged this position see Pressman, "Political Implications of the New Federalism," in Oates, ed., *Financing the New Federalism*, p. 38.

32. Williams, "Federal Objectives and Local Accountability," in Sneed and Waldhorn, eds., *Restructuring the Federal System*, pp. 129-130.

33. The argument about Congress's positive desire to do casework and to attack federal agencies is a central thesis in Morris P. Fiorina, *Congress: Keystone of the Washington Establishment* (New Haven: Yale University Press, 1977).

34. See, David R. Mayhew, *Congress: The Electoral Connection* (New Haven: Yale University Press, 1974).

35. Henry Friendly, *The Federal Administrative Agencies: The Need for Better Definition of Standards* (Cambridge, Mass.: Harvard Univ. Press, 1962); and Theodore J. Lowi, *The End of Liberalism: The Second Republic of the United States*, 2nd Edition, (New York: W.W. Norton & Co., 1979), pp. 92-126.

36. Richard Weatherley and Michael Lipsky, "Street-Level Bureaucrats and Institutional Reform: Implementing Special-Education Reform," *Harvard Educational Review* 47 (1977):196-197. ©1977 by the President and Fellows of Harvard College. Reprinted by permission.

37. For a good example of a policy where federal influence was substantial see Floyd E. Stoner, "Federal Auditors as Regulators: The Case of Title I of ESEA," in Judith V. May and Aaron B. Wildavsky, eds., *The Policy Cycle* (Beverly Hills: Sage Publications, 1978), pp. 199-214.

38. Walker, "A New Intergovernmental System in 1977," p. 112.

39. For a lucid discussion of this problem see Ripley, *The Politics of Economic and Human Resource Development*, pp. 173-174.

40. For a fine discussion of the incentives that work against oversight and concern for problems of policy implementation see Erwin C. Hargrove, *The Missing Link: The Study of the Implementation of Social Policy* (Washington, D C.: The Urban Institute, 1975), pp. 110-115.

41. Fiorina, *Congress*, p. 71.

42. Bardach, *The Implementation Game*, pp. 250-266.

Index

Advisory Commission on Intergovernmental Relations, U.S. (ACIR), 4, 30-31, 110, 154, 163

Alabama syndrome, defined, 148. *See also* Federal role

Ambiguous legislation: benefit distribution and, 128, 157; brought about by inadequate knowledge, 162; citizen participation and, 141; congressional influence and, 149; Congressmen's goals and, 161; executive branch support for, 162; the need for, 162; and program design, 151; redistributive policy and, 161-162; state and local government support for, 162. *See also* Congress; Policy Standards and Resources

Area Redevelopment Act of 1961, 62

Bach, Victor, 127, 131-132

Bardach, Eugene, 148

Barnes, William, 92-93. *See also* Targeting federal aid

Baumer, Donald, 85, 91. *See also* Ohio State University—CETA Study

Bechtal, William, 65

Benefit distribution: and ambiguous legislation, 128, 157; of CDBG, 122-132; of CDBG compared to categorical programs, 126-127, 157; of CETA, 87-96; of CETA compared to categorical programs, 88-90; of CETA Public Service Employment programs, compared to Title I programs, 90; Department of Labor's effect on, 93, 158; direct versus indirect, 13; of GRS, 49-50; HUD's effect on CDBG's, 114, 123, 129, 130, 146, 148, 158; in New Federalism programs, 155-161; policy issues of, defined, 12-13; and redistributive policies, 161-162; sociospatial method for measuring,

123-127. *See also* Congress; Low-income groups; Redistributive policy

Block grants, 2-4, 38. *See also* Categorical grants-in-aid; Decategorization; Grants-in-aid

Brookings Institution, 31, 32, 35, 36, 37, 40, 41, 44, 50, 51, 53, 67, 85, 86, 87, 108, 111, 112, 116, 118-119, 123, 125, 126, 128, 130, 131

Brooks, Jack, 27

Brown, Garry, 110-111

Browning, Rufus, 127, 131

Caputo, David, 53

Carter, Jimmy, 123, 130, 150, 159; and benefit distribution, 146, 158; on federalism, 2; on GRS, 38; impact on CETA, 72, 74; impact on General Revenue Sharing, 33, 36; on targeting federal aid to low-income groups, 5

Categorical grants-in-aid; and benefit distribution, 159; for comunity development, 102-103; criticized, 3-4, 12, 24, 62-64, 76, 103-104; defined, 3; for employment and training programs, 62-63; praised, 38. *See also* Block grants; Decategorization; Decentralization; Grants-in-aid; Recategorization

Citizen participation: and benefit distribution, 95; 132, 159; in CDBG, 108, 110-112, 114, 115; in CETA, 70-71; effect on implementation, 17-18; and elected officials, 37, 75, 116, 141, 142, 143; in GRS, 28, 32, 37, 53; in GRS, CETA, and CDBG, compared, 140-146; impact of, on program reform and expenditures, 53, 122, 153; and Model Cities, 103, 110, 112, 114, 116, 132; role of public hearings in, 145, 153; strengthened through reauthoriza-

About the Author

Carl E. Van Horn is assistant professor of political science at the Eagleton Institute of Politics, Rutgers University, where he teaches and conducts research in the fields of policy analysis and intergovernmental relations. He has also taught at the State University of New York at Stony Brook, where he directed the masters program in public affairs. He received the B.A. from the University of Pittsburgh and the M.A. and Ph.D. in political science from Ohio State University. While at Ohio State he was a research associate at the Mershon Center, where he worked on several major studies of employment and training programs sponsored by the U.S. Department of Labor. His articles on policy analysis, intergovernmental relations, and the Congress have appeared in the *Public Administration Review, Policy Analysis,* the *Journal of Politics,* the *Journal of Human Resources, Administration and Society, Political Methodology,* and various collections.